THE NEGLECTED TRANSITION

The Neglected Transition

BUILDING A RELATIONAL HOME FOR CHILDREN
ENTERING FOSTER CARE

Monique B. Mitchell

OXFORD
UNIVERSITY PRESS

OXFORD
UNIVERSITY PRESS

Oxford University Press is a department of the University of Oxford. It furthers the University's objective of excellence in research, scholarship, and education by publishing worldwide. Oxford is a registered trade mark of Oxford University Press in the UK and certain other countries.

Published in the United States of America by Oxford University Press
198 Madison Avenue, New York, NY 10016, United States of America.

Library of Congress Cataloging-in-Publication Data
Names: Mitchell, Monique B., author.
Title: The neglected transition : building a relational home for children entering foster care / Monique B. Mitchell, Ph.D.
Description: Oxford ; New York : Oxford University Press, [2016] |
Includes bibliographical references and index.
Identifiers: LCCN 2015045959 | ISBN 9780199371174 (alk. paper)
Subjects: LCSH: Foster children. | Foster home care. | Child welfare. |
Social work with children.
Classification: LCC HV873 .M57 2016 | DDC 649/.145—dc23
LC record available at http://lccn.loc.gov/2015045959

9 8 7 6 5 4 3 2
Printed by Webcom, Canada

To all of the courageous children who voiced their stories—your insights, experiences, and unique contributions will be the impetus of healing for many children in foster care—thank you.

This book is dedicated to every child in foster care who feels afraid and alone. My love for you deepens every day.

Contents

Foreword ix
Preface xi
Acknowledgments xxi

Introduction: Why? What? Where? Who? How? When? 1

1. WHY Do I Have to Leave? 11

2. WHAT Is Foster Care? 28

3. WHERE Are You Taking Me? 38

4. WHO Are These People? 50

5. How About ME? 63

6. WHEN Can I Go Home? 78

7. Building a Relational Home for Children's Experiences of Loss, Ambiguity, and Trauma in Foster Care 95

APPENDIX A: A VALUE MODEL OF C.A.R.E.: A BLUEPRINT
    FOR BUILDING A RELATIONAL HOME 101
APPENDIX B: A PHENOMENOLOGICAL JOURNEY: PHILOSOPHICAL
    AND METHODOLOGICAL CONSIDERATIONS 103

APPENDIX C: THE NEGLECTED TRANSITION: C.A.R.E.
    CHECKLIST 111
APPENDIX D: HEALING AFFIRMATIONS FOR CHILDREN
    AND YOUTH IN FOSTER CARE 119

REFERENCES 121
FIGURE CREDITS 125

Foreword

I FIRST MET Monique Mitchell in 2010 at a conference in Miami on loss and grief. She was excited and eager to talk about a book she was writing for practitioners who care for foster children. It was based on her recent research on children's experiences of ambiguity in foster care. She said that my work on ambiguous loss had a significant impact on her research; it provided a guiding theory. We discussed how foster children have multiple ambiguous losses: their own family of parents and siblings, their foster family or families, and finally everyone, because they are often obliged to leave at age 18, often with no contact after. Their loss of family and home became even more ambiguous.

An ambiguous loss is an unclear loss, one in which the entity lost is still physically present somewhere; no one has died. The child knows his or her parents are still alive someplace but he or she cannot get to them. The child may even have siblings but have no or minimal contact with them. Often, children do not know why they were taken away from their own family, which adds to their ambiguity of loss. Being uprooted from one's own family and then having to pass through a string of foster families is immensely stressful and anxiety-producing for foster kids.

Until Monique Mitchell's research and this book that is based on it, no one has so elegantly and specifically linked the problem of ambiguity with fostering. No one has addressed the particular stressor of ambiguous loss so explicitly for foster children. Indeed, ambiguity may well be the most troubling factor for foster kids. If acknowledged and labeled explicitly, it would be easier for foster kids to thrive and manage. Identifying the problem is the entire first step in the process of coping.

Being a foster child or youth is no easy role, as Dr. Mitchell's book will show, but we also hear the stories of resilience, what works, and how foster children can grow up well. We learn all this from the words of the kids themselves, a wonderful gift from the author, who resisted transforming their words into academic summaries.

What we know about the theory of ambiguous loss, the theory that inspired Dr. Mitchell's research and this book, is that it blocks the search for meaning in loss. Not having enough information about why they were removed from their family and home, about when they may be reunited, and still knowing their biological parents are alive somewhere, foster children are caught in a limbo of "not knowing." This is the utmost cause of anxiety and fear. They cannot make sense of their lives, or know who is there for them and who is not. Their loss goes unnoticed as a loss (because no one has died) and thus their grief is also unnoticed. They cannot grieve the loss of "living" family members, or simply a home or their own bed, because society and the professional community have thus far not recognized that their losses are real, even if ambiguous.

Foster children need more information to make sense of it all. And making sense of their situation is essential for lowering their stress and anxiety. Without meaning, the children have no hope, and hope they must have in order to live good and healthy lives. What the rest of us need to remember is that the ambiguity is the culprit, not the foster child.

I leave it to the expertise of Dr. Monique Mitchell to make proposals for improvement to the policymakers and counselors and foster families themselves. In this book, she begins the task of educating us all. She wisely gives us the exact words of the foster children she interviewed, so we hear their voices as they ask us to please help them make their situation better.

Dr. Mitchell's work is the first to link the plight of foster children with the stressor of ambiguity, and thus this book is groundbreaking. She provides a new view of the problem. Foster kids know that the ambiguity, like the elephant in the room, is a source of pain and stress; they know it is there, but we must give it a name so they can deal with it. It is time to label what they already know: foster children have a heap of ambiguous loss.

For all concerned—professionals, policymakers, educators, therapists and counselors, medical practitioners, and the kids themselves—recognizing ambiguity as the real problem is the first step to making life better for foster children. Monique Mitchell's book leads the way.

Pauline Boss

December 24, 2014

Minneapolis, MN

Pauline Boss, Professor Emeritus
Department of Family Social Science
College of Education, Human Development and Social Work
University of Minnesota
Minneapolis, MN

Preface

The journey of life is full of twists and turns. There is laughter and joy, sadness and tears. Our interpretations of experiences define our realities and can shape how we approach our past, our present, and our future. We are faced with choices, make decisions in light of our perceptions and interpretations, open doors, shut doors, create doors, and do our best to navigate ourselves along the way. In life's journey there are many paths, and this book is one path to explore the transition into foster care. Each path is valuable, meaningful, and worth exploring. Our journey will focus specifically on children's experiences of loss, grief, and ambiguity and will present healing suggestions for building a relational home and assisting children as they navigate their way into the foster care system. In this preface, I discuss the book's features and framework, present some of its limitations, and identify the considerations present in other paths to healing.

THE AUDIENCE

This book has been written primarily for child welfare providers (e.g., case managers, foster parents, group home staff, and court-appointed advocates)—that is, the people who are directly involved in the lives of children entering foster care. The experiences provided in this book tap into the various nuances of the transition into foster care and ways that caregivers can C.A.R.E. for children and their experiences of loss and ambiguity as children enter and navigate their way into the foster care system (see Appendix A). Children provide us with clear examples of how to Communicate with them effectively; Affirm their strengths, potential, and worth; Recognize and acknowledge the needs, experiences, and aspirations that are significant to them; and Ensure that their needs of safety, permanency, and well-being are met. Healing suggestions are presented throughout the book to offer care providers guidance and direction from children who have directly experienced the transition into foster care.

Policymakers, academics, and students can also benefit from listening to these children's voices. Research, if applied meaningfully, has the impactful potential to inform practice and policy and further research endeavors. It is my hope that the information found in this book will serve as an impetus for future research studies, the development of much-needed child welfare programs focused specifically on children's experiences of loss and ambiguity in foster care, and enhancements in child welfare policy to address the mental health needs of children in foster care, especially during their transition into foster care. Ultimately, however, the voices of all parties (e.g., children, caregivers, practitioners, academics, policymakers, etc.) should be considered to determine best practices, program enhancement, and policy needs.

THE AUTHOR

You never quite forget the day your world shatters. Feelings of confusion, shock, denial, guilt, and so many others cycle in your mind. When I was separated from my family during my adolescence, I couldn't quite make sense of what, who, where, when, why, and how. What was going to happen to me? Who was going to be there for me? Where was I going to go? When would my family be together again? Why was this all happening? And that ever-pressing question, which I repeatedly asked myself: how was I going to get through this?

My phone just rang. One of my family members has died. I am miles from home, in another country, consumed in writing this book, and, in the midst of it all, I did not get a chance to say goodbye. It's interesting how life works, how in any given second loss can occur—without notice, without preparation. I cannot help but consider the synchronicity of it all—this event occurring exactly as I am writing about my experiences of loss and ambiguity. Another experience of loss and ambiguity confronts me on my journey and waits for a response. I sit here and try to make meaning of what just occurred. Is my family OK? How are they handling this? Shouldn't I be going home? Is this really happening? I can't help but think about how many children are out there right now, asking the same questions.

Although my experiences inspire me to assist others whose worlds have been shattered by similar events, this book is not about me or my journey. It is about courageous children who were willing to be vulnerable and share their stories to help others in a similar situation. This book is about children who believe that change is possible and that their voices can inspire change. These children's voices far supersede mine. I simply serve as a means to bring their voices to the forefront.

As we move forward in this book, we will explore children's experiences as they have described them. Their reports have been kept intact in order to capture the essence of their words, their feelings, their interpretations, and their expression. Although there is no way I could fully capture the experience of hearing from these children directly—just merely being in their presence is a humbling experience—I have made every effort to portray their voices and experiences as authentically as possible.

It is important for me to note that, as an academic, an educator, and a practitioner, there are multiple languages and approaches from which I could have chosen to write this book. From my experience of educating (and being educated by) hundreds of child welfare professionals, I have learned that it is not academic language or an adult's expert knowledge that interests or captivates my audience's attention; rather, and most appropriately, it is the children's voices and experiences that are valued the most. This awareness humbles and reminds me that I am in a privileged position where I have the rare opportunity to convey and communicate the voices of children to multitudes of people, locally and globally, who are invested in hearing what *children* have to say. Contrary to my position, most children in foster care cannot readily or conveniently access a platform where their voices can be amplified. The children in this book have courageously shared their voices with me in an effort to contribute to meaningful change in the lives of other children in foster care. As such, I consider it both a privilege and a responsibility to convey to others what I have learned from children about the transition into foster care and how to C.A.R.E. for and build a relational home for children entering foster care. I have chosen to fill most of the pages in this book with the children's words, rather than my own academic inferences and applications. My intention is to amplify the voices of children so that readers, using their own knowledge, wisdom, and expertise, can consider the efforts needed within their respective profession or practice to make meaningful change in the lives of children entering foster care. Finally, I would like to emphasize that, although I am certified in thanatology (the scientific study of death, dying, and bereavement) and conduct research that has many clinical implications, this book is not intended to be used as a substitute for therapy; it is an opportunity to view the journey into foster care from a child's perspective and to consider how to enfranchise and heal children's experiences of loss, grief, and ambiguity during this critical life transition. I am humbled to join you on this journey as children discuss their experiences of loss and ambiguity during the transition into foster care while offering messages of love, healing, and hope along the way.

THE APPROACH

This book is written from a bottom-up, child-centered, strengths-based, emic (insider's) perspective. Children's experiences of loss and ambiguity create a foundation from which their concerns and struggles can be brought to the forefront for meaningful change in practice, policy, and research. The first step in accomplishing this objective (and the intention behind this book) is to pause and listen to children's voices about their experiences of loss and ambiguity during the transition into foster care, the impact of these experiences, and how children and their needs, experiences, and aspirations can be valued during this significant life transition. By focusing exclusively on the child's perspective, child welfare professionals have the opportunity to consider how children in foster care experience loss and ambiguity and the healing actions that can build a relational home. The next step needed to ensure that children's needs are met involves an in-depth evaluation of the policies and practices that address, or fail to address, these experiences; however, this latter approach is beyond the scope of this book. Because policies and practices can differ from state to state and country to country, it is hoped that child welfare experts (e.g., policymakers, researchers, and practitioners) will consider the experiences and needs of children as they enter foster care and whether these needs are adequately being addressed by the respective policies, practices, and research that guide their work. Because the youth voice should be at the forefront of systems change, it is hoped that the experiences and advice reported by children in this book will serve as a catalyst to guide child welfare professionals in their efforts to meaningfully C.A.R.E. for children as they transition into foster care.

THE FRAMEWORK

Phenomenology, the study of understanding the nature of being and an individual's life world, is the philosophical foundation that guides the methodological framework of this book (see Appendix B). It involves meaning-making and an investigation into how a population experiences a particular phenomenon. Therefore, children's reports will serve as the lens through which we engage their world and experiences.

Ambiguous loss (Boss, 1999), the assumptive world (Janoff-Bulman, 1989; Kauffman, 2002; Parkes, 1971), disenfranchised grief (Doka, 1989), and cognitive appraisals (Lazarus & Folkman, 1984) are the theories that inform our journey.

Other researchers, operating from differing methodologies, philosophies, and theories, have identified alternate frameworks to examine foster care phenomena, such as bio-ecological or developmental stage models (Boyd Webb, 2006; Fahlberg, 1991). Although this book is not guided by attachment theory or developmental models, I encourage readers to consider and explore how developmental approaches can be utilized to meet the needs of grieving children during specific developmental periods. These books include, but are not limited to, *A Child's Journey Through Placement* (Fahlberg, 1991), *Working with Traumatized Youth in Child Welfare* (Boyd Webb, 2006), and *Grief and Loss: Theories and Skills for the Helping Professions* (Walsh, 2012).

THE EXPERTS

An expert is defined as "a person who has special skill or knowledge in some particular field" (dictionary.com). The purpose of this book is to explore, acknowledge, and address children's experiences of loss and ambiguity as they transition into foster care. Therefore, consistent with a phenomenological framework, the children themselves are considered the experts on this phenomenon, and their voices constitute the main authorship of this book. The questions posed and the healing suggestions offered throughout the book are based on children's reports, reflections, and contributions.

The intentional focus on the child's perspective also assists in balancing the power dynamics of authorship in current child welfare literature, which often represents solely the adult perspective. This being said, there is value in considering the perspectives of all experts who experience any given phenomenon. Other avenues to explore the transition into foster care include examining the perspectives of care providers and how they experience a child's transition into foster care, as well as experiences of loss and ambiguity as a result of being involved in the child welfare system (e.g., when a child leaves a caregiver's residence, when a child is removed from a case manager's caseload, and when a family is preparing for the arrival of a child from foster care). As a complement to the children's voices presented in this book, I encourage readers to seek out books, academic journal articles, technical papers, and other resources that capture experiences of loss and ambiguity by care providers and others in the child welfare system (e.g., Edelstein, Burge, & Waterman, 2001; Riggs & Willsmore, 2012; Simpson, 2012).

THE BREADTH

Although I have made efforts to capture most of the experiences that children addressed in their interviews as stressful or traumatic, it is important to note that the information elicited from these interviews may not capture all of the stressful and traumatic experiences in relation to this phenomenon. Additional research is always necessary to continue learning about children's perceptions of their experiences and ways we can better meet their needs during their transition into the foster care system. It is also important to note that the experiences presented in this book capture children's initial experiences of entering foster care and, therefore, experiences of loss, grief, ambiguity, stress, and trauma throughout a child's placement in foster care are not addressed. These experiences should also be acknowledged and taken into account.

THE VOICES

The voices and experiences of children derive from three main sources: children in an original research study, expert consultants on youth advisory boards, and reports of youth participant feedback in other research studies.

Original Research Study

Twenty children in regular non-kinship foster care, 8 to 15 years-old, participated in the original research study (see Table 1). The average time spent in care was 20 months. On average, children experienced two placements within 3 years of being in care.

The participants were recruited from a Children's Aid Society agency in a central province in Canada. The agency was located in a mid-sized city with close proximity to rural communities. Four criteria were required for participant eligibility

TABLE 1
Demographic Characteristics of Study Sample

Characteristic	Number	Percent
Age		
8–11	7	35
12–15	13	65
Gender		
Female	11	55
Male	9	45
Length of Time in Care		
6 months–1 year	5	25
1 year–2 years	9	45
2 years–3 years	6	30

in the study: (1) foster care status—regular foster care; (2) age—8 to 15 years old; (3) duration in foster care—more than 6 months and less than 3 years; and (4) placement type—non-kinship foster care (see Appendix B for additional details regarding these criteria). The total number of participants in the sample was based on the sample principle of representativeness (Patterson & Williams, 2002); therefore, all children at the agency who met the study criteria were invited to participate in the study. All names and identifying information have been changed in this book to protect the children who participated in the study. The children's ages, at the time of their reports, have remained intact.

Children participated in two phases of the study: a rapport-building group workshop (phase one) and individual semi-structured interviews (phase two). Both phases of the data collection were held in classrooms at the researcher's university. All data was collected during phase two of the research study, which occurred a few weeks after phase one. The interviews were held in a private room and ranged from 30 to 60 minutes in length. Children were reminded of the purpose of the study and their individual rights as a research participant (e.g., the right to decline answering any question, the right to decline to participate in the study at any time, etc.). Lines of inquiry addressed children's appraisals of the initial entrance into care, the reason for their foster care placement, assistance offered, or not offered, to them during their placement in foster care, their initial experiences of placement in the foster home, and additional experiences that participants interpreted as stressful or benign-positive. Toward the end of the interview, children were invited to offer advice about the transition into foster care that could be shared with children transitioning into foster care, care providers, and case managers. All children received a verbal debriefing about the study and two free movie passes for their participation. The research study was reviewed and approved by an institutional review board at a Canadian university. For additional information about the research methodology and data analysis, please refer to Appendix B and/or the academic journal articles published on this research (Mitchell & Kuczynski, 2010; Mitchell, Kuczynski, Tubbs, & Ross, 2010).

Limitations

It is important to note that the experiences of children under the age of 8 were not part of the original research and, as a result, are not captured in this book. The transition experiences of children during all developmental stages (i.e., infancy, early childhood, middle childhood, adolescence, and early adulthood) are valuable and deserve attention and consideration. It is hoped that future research will explore younger children's experiences of the transition into foster care and the unique approaches needed to attend to their specific needs.

Because the study examined children's experiences of placement into non-kinship foster care, the experiences of grief, loss, and ambiguity by children transitioning into kinship foster care are not captured. Therefore, some of the ambiguous domains that are outlined in this book (e.g., placement context ambiguity and relationship ambiguity) may not be as applicable for children who are placed into kinship placements as they are for children in non-kinship foster care.

Children in the research sample mostly discussed their experiences of transitioning into a foster home and not a group home. Therefore, children who enter foster care and are placed into group homes may have other experiences of loss and ambiguity that are not captured by these interviews. Further research in this area would be valuable. Nevertheless, all children who enter foster care are likely to experience loss and ambiguity on some level, regardless of whether they are placed with relatives, strangers, in a foster home, or a group home.

Although children in foster care have many needs that require the attention and nurturance of adults (e.g., physical, emotional, psychological, spiritual, educational, and material needs), the needs that stem from loss and ambiguity are the primary focus of this book. Therefore, other needs that are essential must also be considered to C.A.R.E. for the overall well-being of children.

Finally, it is also important to note that none of the children who participated in the study had physical disabilities. Research that focuses specifically on the experiences of children with special needs and disabilities during the transition into foster care is much needed.

Expert Consultants on Youth Advisory Boards

In my current position, I regularly communicate with advisory members about practices, initiatives, and research in the state that can affect and/or involve children in foster care. Advisory members provide feedback on child welfare policies, practice, and/or research and are well-versed in providing constructive feedback to care providers; that is, advisors receive training on how to provide feedback to child welfare professionals that is productive, encouraging, and helpful, as well as how to critically reflect on, identify, and make suggestions for needed changes to enhance and improve service delivery. When the members of the advisory boards learned that I was writing a book on children's experiences of the transition into foster care, they expressed interest in learning what children in foster care had to say. In response to their request, time was set aside in one of their advisory meetings to discuss the themes and experiences that emerged from the children's reports. Many of the members stated that they had similar questions when they entered foster care and believed their insights would also be helpful to care providers who were involved in the lives of children transitioning into foster care. Because their request to contribute feedback was within the scope of their advisory roles and responsibilities, members who wanted to contribute to the book were invited to provide feedback and advice on the themes and questions raised by the children in the original research study.

Eleven advisory board members, 18 to 23 years-old, contributed to this book. The advisors' reflections on the emergent themes echoed many of the experiences of the children in the research study, who were much younger than they and lived in a different country. This is important to note, as it suggests that the questions in this book may be raised by children of various ages and nationalities. As such, the experiences and advice of the expert consultants are interspersed throughout the book to further illustrate experiences of ambiguity and loss during the transition into foster care. The activities involving the expert youth consultants did not constitute research as defined by 45CFR46 and, as such, were exempt from IRB oversight.

Other Research Studies

Research studies involving children and youth as participants are also referenced to address other children's experiences of ambiguity, loss, and/or the transition into foster care. For example, research by Fahlberg (1991), Herrick and Piccus (2005), Unrau, Seita, and Putney (2009), and Whiting and Lee (2003) provide insider knowledge about children's experiences in foster care. Although these studies did not focus specifically on children's experiences of the transition into foster care, each study includes reports by children that illustrate their experiences of loss and/ or ambiguity while in the foster care system. These findings further suggest that children experience loss and ambiguity in foster care and validate the importance of attending to these experiences.

On a final note, what I have found particularly interesting is that, regardless of the child's nationality (i.e., American or Canadian) or age (with the exception of those who entered foster care at infancy), most children and youth with whom I have spoken or have heard speak about their experiences in foster care vividly remember entering their first foster care placement and how they were impacted by this experience. As will be demonstrated, the questions posed by children in this book have been raised and affirmed by other children and youth in research studies, children and youth on advisory boards, and alumni of foster care when reflecting on their transition into foster care. This being said, the voices of children who experienced foster care in Canada, the United States, or the United Kingdom are the dominant voices in this book and may differ from the perceptions and interpretations of children entering foster care in other countries.

THE IMPACT OF THE TRANSITION INTO FOSTER CARE

Although the majority of children in the study reported experiencing the transition into foster care as a significant life transition that resulted in a major shift in their assumptive world, not *all* children will experience the transition into foster care as traumatic or stressful; some children feel relieved when they are placed in foster care. Therefore, it is very important to speak to children about their perceptions before making any inferences about how they are interpreting their experience and, subsequently, determining the best approach to support them as they transition into foster care. This being said, most children will experience a significant shift in their inner and interpersonal life as a result of being placed in foster care, regardless of whether they interpret the transition into foster care as stressful or benign-positive. When a shift in one's assumptive world occurs, loss, grief, and ambiguity often follow.

Acknowledgments

"A PICTURE IS worth a thousand words." As I reflect on the love that has colored the authoring of this book, I find myself, in this moment, without words. The picture in my mind speaks volumes. In the silence that ushers my mind, I am warmed by thoughts of all the children and youth who made this book possible. It is their wisdom, introspection, and courage that, ultimately, breathe life into the words on these pages. Through their experiences, these children paint a vision of hope, a masterpiece of care, enfranchisement, and healing.

I cannot help but smile when I consider all the people who, in their own unique way, contributed to the development of this book. My family and friends who lovingly encouraged me during every step of the process; reminding me that I, too, am not alone and that love transcends time and space—and, yes, dad, the picture is now painted! I am grateful for colleagues, staff, students, and youth advisors who enthusiastically shared in my excitement and insisted they must have a personal copy of the book even before reading the words that would color these pages. I have no doubt that their love and support was fueled by their shared vision of a picture that was worth a thousand healing words. I am grateful for their faith and belief in this book's message.

I contemplate how it took many fortnights and heartfelt years to develop this book. I am appreciative of all those who consulted on the research from which this book is based (Dr. Leon Kuczynski, Dr. Carolyn Tubbs, Dr. Christopher Ross, Dr. John Russon, and Dr. Sandra Mackey) and the child welfare agency staff who generously supported me in my pursuit to capture the lived experience of children as they transition into the foster care system. I am also extremely grateful to the youth and young adults on the state youth advisory boards (you know who you are!) who contributed meaningful feedback to the contents of the book and the coloring of these pages. You inspire me beyond words.

Toni M. Jones, it goes without being said that you are an editor extraordinaire. Thank you for agreeing to use your detailed paintbrush to touch up and brighten my picture, confirming and affirming that light and love shine through.

Finally, I give thanks for the bursts of inspiration and reverie that continuously awaken me in the wee hours of the night—forever assuring me that many mediums exist to communicate love and healing. I am humbled by the constant reminder that I am just one of many scribes who author the colorful nuances of life.

THE NEGLECTED TRANSITION

Introduction

WHY? WHAT? WHERE? WHO? HOW? WHEN?

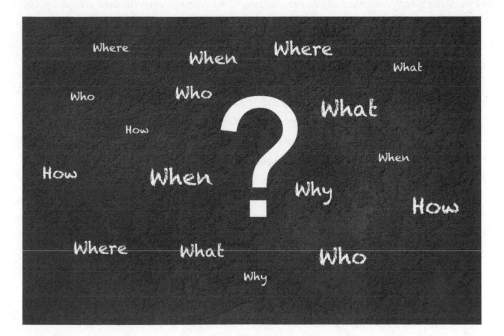

AN INTRODUCTION TO LOSS AND AMBIGUITY DURING
THE TRANSITION INTO FOSTER CARE

Abigail's Story

Abigail[1] was 10 and a half when she entered foster care. Although it happened a year and a half ago, Abigail still remembers the exact month and day that she transitioned into foster care and how she felt at that time. "I remember it like it was yesterday." Abigail shared, "It was May 2nd. It was a Friday, or it was a Saturday. Actually, I'm pretty sure it was a Friday, and I wasn't happy."

On Friday, May 2nd, Abigail was playing with some of her friends when all of a sudden a strange woman approached her. The woman told Abigail that she was going to be placed in foster care, immediately. Abigail was confused and angry because no one had told her earlier that she had to move into foster care, and she did not understand what was happening. The woman put Abigail in a car and drove her home. When Abigail got out of the car, she found someone else packing her stuff into a car and wondered what was going on. She ran into the house and asked her mom what was happening. Abigail heard the strange woman say to her mother, "I'm going to have to take Abigail." The woman turned to Abigail and said, "Abigail, you're going to have to come with us." and then looked at Abigail's mom and said, "You know why." Abigail thought, "What the heck is she talking about? What is this lady doing in my house, and why is she telling my mom she knows exactly why I am going into this weirdo's car? OK, somebody fill me in before I get angry. Why is this lady talking to my mom in that kind of tone?" When Abigail asked her mom if she was going to come with her, her mother replied, "I'm not coming with you because you are going into foster care." Abigail asked, "What is that?" Her mom responded, "Where people take care of you because I can't."

Abigail felt like she was being kidnapped. Everything happened so quickly. Most of her stuff had been packed, but there were a few things she was unable to bring along. Abigail was sad and angry about having to leave. She ran into the car, found her pillow and screamed into it. Although she expressed reluctance about leaving, Abigail soon discovered that she had no choice in the matter. In the absence of her mother, she was being driven away from her home by a strange woman who called herself a social services worker, whoever that is! While in the car, Abigail thought to herself, "Does anybody know what's going on other than mom and this weirdo? What's happening?" In silence, Abigail sat in the car questioning where she was going, the meaning of "foster care," who the people were that she was about to meet, what would happen once she got "there," and why this was all happening in the first place.

---

[1] Abigail's Story is a representative amalgam of various children's reports, representing the dominant experiences that emerged from children's stories about the transition into foster care.

A DIFFERENT KIND OF LOSS

When you think of loss and grief, what first comes to mind? The physical death of a loved one? A recent burial or memorial of someone you love? The death of your childhood pet? Perhaps your body begins to stir up feelings that are often associated with loss and grief. Do you sense sadness? Despair? Denial? Anger? Perhaps confusion?

Discussions or acknowledgments of loss and grief in society are usually centered on the physical death of an individual; that is, the individual is physically deceased, and there will no longer be an opportunity to see, hear, or speak with that person again. In Western society, we have been conditioned to believe and acknowledge that the primary precipitator of loss and grief is the physical death of someone whom we love, care for, and/or know. How then do we explain those moments when the emotions associated with death arise within us, yet there is no physical death to which we can attribute these emotions? Do you recall a time in your life when you felt extreme sadness, despair, or confusion about an event that did not involve someone dying? Although it was not someone's death that triggered these emotions, did you feel overwhelmed with emotion, as if someone or something *had died* during this time? Perhaps it was a divorce? Or when your child took those big steps and decided to move out of the family home? Perhaps when you lost a job or a home? Or maybe when your pet ran away and never returned? Do these experiences count? How would you feel if these events were considered "unimportant" by the people you love and depend upon? How would you feel if the losses that overwhelmed you with grief were not considered significant losses at all? Although these losses may not receive the same degree of acknowledgment by society as a physical death, these experiences of loss and grief may be as important as, nearly as important as, or more important than those experiences of loss due to a physical death. Sadly, those who experience these types of non-death losses may also experience *disenfranchised grief* (Doka, 1989)—that is, grief that is neglected or left unattended because the loss is not acknowledged or recognized by society as significant.

In this book, we will explore the significant losses that precipitate disenfranchised grief and the types of ambiguity that children experience as a result of being placed in the foster care system. We will focus on the types of losses that rarely are acknowledged yet can leave deep emotional scars and impede a child's healthy socio-emotional development. A space will be created where children's voices, fears, and concerns can be heard, and suggestions will be made about ways to C.A.R.E. for children's experiences of loss and ambiguity as they transition into the child welfare system.

AMBIGUITY AND LOSS: THE SILENT STRESSORS

When individuals are presented with a new event or situation, they are naturally inclined to think about how it may benefit or threaten their well-being (Lazarus & Folkman, 1984). Decisions are made about how to move forward and interact with others based on one's personal assessment of the situation. What happens then when someone has conflicting information or not enough information to determine if an event or situation is in his or her best interest? The individual experiences *ambiguity*.

Ambiguity is a silent stressor that has the ability to create emotional turmoil and unrest (Cowan, 1991). When children are unable to determine how a situation may affect their well-being, that is, when they experience ambiguity, they may become overwhelmed with feelings of confusion, fear, and stress. When individuals are faced with situations that they interpret as ambiguous, they more often expect negative outcomes than they do positive outcomes (Chow & Sarin, 2002). Situations that are perceived as ambiguous can contribute to feelings of tension, anxiety, and depression.

Loss occurs when an individual is deprived of or being without something or someone of value. Grief is a natural reaction to loss (DeSpelder & Strickland, 2010). As with ambiguity, grief can leave us with an overwhelming sense of confusion, disorganization, anxiety, rage, resentment, sadness, longing, and loneliness. The suppression of grief or being overwhelmed with grief can contribute to poor adjustment to the situations and events that precipitate loss (DeSpelder & Strickland, 2010). Countless articles and books have addressed the negative impacts that can occur when grief is left unattended (Boss, 2006; Doka, 1989; Levine, 2006; Neimeyer, 2001). These impacts include, but are not limited to, guilt, post-traumatic stress disorder, isolation, substance abuse, anxiety, low self-esteem, and despair. To explore all of the effects of unattended grief is well beyond the scope of this book; however, what is important to note is that there is consensus among grief experts that individuals who are experiencing loss need support and comfort to assist them as they deal with their grief (Silverman, 2004), and failure to attend to children's experiences of grief can result in negative short- and long-term outcomes.

LOSS AND THE TRANSITION INTO FOSTER CARE

Consider this scenario. You are a child who lives in a home with your parents and siblings. Although your family life isn't perfect, the thought of losing your parents and siblings terrifies you. One day your worst nightmare comes true. Without much information or preparation, you are removed from your home and told that you won't be returning for some time. Left behind are your parents, your siblings, your friends, your home, your bedroom, your fish tank, your favorite stuffed animal, your book report due on Monday (your mind races, "I am in so much trouble. My teacher is going to be so angry with me!"), and other things of importance that you can't even think about right now. You are in shock. You are confused. You are scared.

The transition into foster care is fraught with experiences of loss. Children experience a loss of home, a loss of stability and consistency, a loss of important relationships, a loss of identity—significant losses that can create confusion and emotional turmoil. The events that trigger loss, ambiguity, and grief, which usually occur within a very short period of time and leave little to no time for children to process what is happening, will be explored in the first chapter. Unfortunately, how children experience the initial placement into foster care and how this experience can negatively affect children's well-being has received very little attention in policy, practice, and research.

As we journey through this book, we will uncover how children are impacted by the events that occur as a result of being placed in foster care. The various tangible and intangible losses experienced by children will be highlighted, including losses of their home, personal belongings, family, friends, pets, school, and identity. By identifying these silent losses, we can better assist children by acknowledging the losses they experience and illuminating ways to heal grief.

AMBIGUITY AND THE TRANSITION INTO FOSTER CARE

The significant events of loss that children experience as a result of being placed in foster care often precipitate ambiguity (Mitchell, 2008). Children will experience ambiguity when they have no information, too little information, or too much conflicting information to make sense of how an event will impact their personal well-being (Mitchell, 2008). In the context of children's initial entry into foster care, children have been found to experience various types of ambiguity. Children may experience *placement reason ambiguity* (i.e., a lack of clarity about the reason for being placed in foster care), *structural ambiguity* (i.e., a lack of clarity about the meaning of foster care), *placement context ambiguity* (i.e., a lack of clarity about the context of the foster home), *temporal ambiguity* (i.e., a lack of clarity about the duration of the foster care placement), *relationship ambiguity* (i.e., a lack of clarity about the people with whom they will be placed), *ambiguous loss* (i.e., a lack of clarity about the psychological and/or physical presence of members of their psychological family; Boss, 1999), and *role ambiguity* (i.e., a lack of clarity about one's role within familial contexts). As we move forward in our journey, we will explore these various types of ambiguity, how children in foster care interpret and experience ambiguity, and identify ways to assist children in healing from experiences of loss and ambiguity.

LOSS, AMBIGUITY, AND TRAUMA

The information provided in this book is trauma informed; that is, it takes into consideration the experiences that can be traumatic for children as they transition into the foster care system. It is important to note that these experiences shed light on only a fraction of the trauma spectrum. In other words, the experiences of loss and ambiguity provide an opportunity for us to consider how children experience trauma, but by no means provide a comprehensive trauma framework. There are many different events and transactions that may be traumatizing to a child beyond the experiences of loss and ambiguity. Therefore, I offer one approach to exploring children's experiences of trauma in the child welfare system while simultaneously acknowledging that trauma can occur on many different levels and in many different ways.

Although many facets of children's experiences of loss, ambiguity, and trauma during the transition into foster care will be discussed, this book by no means exhaustively portrays all of their experiences. It does, however, shed light on numerous ways that loss, grief, and ambiguity are manifested in children's lives. By listening to the stories shared by children, it is hoped that care providers will assess the impact of loss, ambiguity, and trauma, and how these silent stressors have the potential to shatter a child's assumptive world.

ENFRANCHISING THE PIECES: ACKNOWLEDGING
A CHILD'S SHATTERED ASSUMPTIVE WORLD

Unfortunately, as will be illustrated by children's reports, certain events and their traumatic impact on children go unrecognized and unattended all too often by the adults in their world. A child's assumptive world[2] can shatter when she or he is placed in foster care. Children's understandings of *who, what, where, when, why,* and *how* in regard to their understanding of existence and the world around them becomes compromised and tenaciously challenged. Each chapter in this book highlights the pieces of a child's assumptive world that shatter as a result of entering foster care. Fortunately, as will be demonstrated by the wisdom of children's experiences, insights, and advice, a blueprint can be created to enfranchise children's experiences of loss and ambiguity and facilitate C.A.R.E. and healing.

---

[2] Please refer to Appendix B for the theoretical discussion regarding this construct.

In Chapter 1, our journey begins in a child's original home, before his or her placement into foster care. Children recall their experiences of being notified about the need to be placed into foster care, the reason for their placement in foster care, placement reason ambiguity, and their removal from their homes. Healing suggestions to assist children during these vulnerable, and potentially traumatic, transactions are provided.

In Chapter 2, we explore structural ambiguity and how children interpret and make meaning of the foster care system. Children's experiences during the "home transfer" (i.e., the transfer from their original home to their new home in foster care), as well as the benefits of receiving systemic and person-centered information prior to their placement in foster care, are presented and discussed.

In Chapter 3, we examine placement context ambiguity and the concerns and fears that children may experience in relation to their new residence. As will be discussed, many questions can arise for children entering a non-kinship foster care placement because they often do not know where they are going, who lives in the home where they will be residing, and how they will be impacted.

In Chapter 4, our journey continues as we explore relationship ambiguity and children's initial experiences of their foster care placement. In this chapter, children's experiences and perspectives about forming new familial relationships are highlighted, and healing suggestions to assist children in adjusting and adapting to their new home environment are provided.

In Chapter 5, we delve into the inner depths of a child's inner and interpersonal world and reflect on children's experiences of role ambiguity. Children's reports illustrate how their understanding of self can be challenged and transformed as they acclimate to the culture of foster care, and suggest ways that care providers can attend to the psychological, emotional, and spiritual well-being of children during this significant life transition.

In Chapter 6, we explore children's experiences of temporal ambiguity and ambiguous loss. Children's reports reveal how they navigate ambiguous loss and ways that care providers can acknowledge, attend, and enfranchise children's experiences of ambiguous loss, symbolic loss, and disenfranchised grief in the foster care system.

In the final chapter, we conclude our journey by reflecting on the importance of building a relational home for children and their experiences of ambiguity, loss, grief, and trauma in foster care. By enfranchising the events and losses experienced by children that may not be acknowledged or recognized by adults, we care for the significant relationships and experiences of children in foster care and build a relational home for connection and healing.

A BLUEPRINT FOR BUILDING A RELATIONAL HOME FOR CHILDREN ENTERING FOSTER CARE: HEALING EXPERIENCES OF LOSS AND AMBIGUITY

Trauma is constituted in an intersubjective context in which severe emotional pain cannot find a relational home in which it can be held. In such a context, painful affect states become unendurable—that is, traumatic.

STOLOROW (2007, p. 10)

What Is a Relational Home?

Children who are suffering from psychological trauma need a relational home where their emotional pain can be nurtured. In his book *Trauma and Human Existence*, Stolorow (2007) states, "So long as my traumatized states found no relational home within which they could be given voice, they remained largely vegetative in nature" (p. 30). When I first read this statement, I could not help but pause and reflect that, indeed, perhaps building a relational home is key to caring for our children's experiences of loss and ambiguity in the foster care system. Without acknowledgment and support, children may spiral into a shattered world of loneliness, hopelessness, depression, guilt, and despair (Doka, 2002). Ambiguity can also lead to trauma and is often overlooked as a source of trauma (Boss, 2006). In fact, Boss (2006) asserts that ambiguous loss (see Chapter 6) is one of the most "unmanageable and traumatizing" stressors. Children need not feel alone in their grief and confusion. It is for this very reason that this book has been written.

While actively listening to the voices of hundreds of children through research studies and my daily interactions, I have learned that a relational home can only be built for children if their experiences are first enfranchised. In other words, a relational home is a relational space where children's needs, experiences, and aspirations are valued and nurtured by C.A.R.E. (see Appendix A). It involves Communicating with children about their needs and experiences; Affirming children's strengths, potential, and worthiness of unconditional love; Recognizing and acknowledging matters of significance (i.e., needs, experiences, and aspirations); and Ensuring that their needs of safety, permanency, and well-being are met. Children's experiences and suggestions about loss and ambiguity outline a blueprint for building a relational home for children entering foster care, creating a space of love, hope, and healing.

In my daily conversations with child welfare care providers, I have learned that care providers have a lot of responsibilities and a lot of heart. Carrying out their responsibilities can be particularly difficult when there is so much to juggle, so little time, and, all too often, not enough resources to support their efforts. Sometimes it can be difficult to identify which responsibility should take priority when everything seems important, deserving, and needed. I empathize with this experience and can personally attest that many care providers work long hours and invest a lot of time, energy, and love in doing the best that they can with the little resources they have; it is here, in this understanding, where children's voices can offer the guidance to create a much-needed source of support—an insider's perspective on how to build a relational home for children in foster care.

It's easy to become so preoccupied with our everyday lives and responsibilities that we sometimes forget to communicate with children; we may forget to ask children questions, invite children to ask us questions, or simply listen to children about their needs, experiences, or aspirations. What I have learned from children in foster care is that they have a lot of questions when they enter foster care, and they are hoping there will be someone in their life who will provide them with meaningful C.A.R.E. and a relational home—that is, a space where someone will communicate with them, affirm their worth, recognize and acknowledge their needs, experiences, and aspirations, and ensure that these needs are met. What I have learned from care providers is that they are invested in the best interests of the child and, no matter how much they know or have learned, they are always interested in hearing what children have to say and how to care for children in the best way possible; and, it is through this wisdom that a loving space is created and meaningful change and healing occur.

What Is Healing?

Healing is a process, not an outcome. It is not something to be pursued as an ultimate goal, but rather is a process that can propel someone to thrive. Children are constantly confronted by and engaging with life events that have the potential to be interpreted as ambiguous, harmful, and stressful. Although healing is a process that occurs within an individual, it is also a process that is largely influenced by efforts and insights that manifest within one's relational world. It is my hope that this book will serve as a healing resource, and one of many, that care providers can use to walk with children on their journey. Healing, in the context of this phenomenon, is conceptualized as a process of C.A.R.E. that builds a relational home for children as they navigate their way through the child welfare system—a system that will constantly challenge them in terms of loss, grief, and ambiguity.

As we journey through each chapter of the book, it is hoped that care providers will recognize and identify the experiences of loss and ambiguity that can precipitate trauma for children as they transition into foster care and the importance of acknowledging and attending to these significant life experiences. The healing suggestions, when applied meaningfully, can build a relational home that welcomes and nurtures children's experiences of loss and ambiguity. This being said, it is important to keep in mind that each child's journey is unique and every child will have his or her own interests, beliefs, concerns, aspirations, and needs. The healing suggestions presented in this book are suggestions, not recommendations. Each suggestion is intended to be considered and reflected upon in respect to each child's specific situation. Some suggestions may not be applicable or appropriate for every child. Ultimately, the best interests of the child should be a care provider's primary consideration and implementation guide.

A JOURNEY OF LOSS, AMBIGUITY, AND HEALING

As we begin our journey, children courageously guide us on our way, offering wisdom to care providers about how to C.A.R.E. for their traumatic experiences of loss and ambiguity and serve as empowered catalysts of healing.

WHY DO I HAVE TO LEAVE?
What is foster care?
Where are you taking me?
Who are these people?
How about me?
When can I go home?

The questions arise. The answers await us.

"It's like you're being kidnapped and nobody wants to tell you nuttin."
ANGELA, 12 years old

I

WHY Do I Have to Leave?

WELCOME, FELLOW TRAVELER. The first stop in our journey is a child's original home. As we quietly enter the front room of a child's home, we hear the muffled sounds of clothes being stuffed into a suitcase. Our attention is redirected as we pick up on the tension in the air as a group of adults exchange words. As we continue to scan the room, we notice a child who is standing in the midst of it all. We focus in and as our eyes meet, we sense the overwhelming weight of a child's heavy heart.

Being removed from one's home can be a startling and confusing experience, especially for children. Children are often abruptly notified of their need to "leave home" and go "somewhere safe." Although from an adult's perspective, a child's removal from his or her home may seem to be a relatively quick, isolated, one-time event lasting only a matter of hours, this event is a significant turning point in children's lives and one that many children will relive over and over again in their minds. In light of this information, how adults handle a child's removal from the home can have a dramatic impact on a child's initial perceptions of the child welfare system. In this chapter, I will explain how the events associated with notifying and placing children in foster care can leave a lasting impression on children and, later in the book, how children's experiences of these events may influence their adaptations to the new situations and relationships they encounter as they navigate their placement in foster care.

WHAT'S HAPPENING?

Most children are not expecting, nor are they prepared, to leave their families and their homes. Children are often notified abruptly of the need to be removed from their home while their belongings are simultaneously being packed (Mitchell & Kuczynski, 2010; Unrau et al., 2008). Confusion and shock surface as children try to process the sudden news that they "need to leave" immediately!

Children often do not have enough information and very little time to process what is happening, given how abruptly they are removed their homes. Furthermore, they rarely know the people who are telling them that they need to leave their home. Could you imagine arriving home only to find your bags packed, a stranger in your family room, and no choice but to listen and follow the instruction to leave? The impact of this experience receives very little attention in research, policy, and practice, yet it is an experience that often leaves a lasting impression on children.

Derrick's Experience
13 years old

Derrick remembers when he first came into foster care. When asked what foster care was like, Derrick replied that it was "garbage because I couldn't stay living with my parents." Derrick expresses his displeasure with having to leave his home.

Denise's Experience
13 years old

When asked if she remembers when she first moved into her foster home, Denise replies, "Um, I think August 18th, I do believe. Well, I know it was in August. August 18th . . . It was scary because I didn't know anyone." Although Denise had been in care for some time, she could remember the exact month and date that she had entered into foster care. She also recalled how the placement in foster care was scary for her because she did not know anyone. In her account, we can hear an experience of loss (i.e., not having anyone present with whom she was familiar) and ambiguity (i.e., not being familiar with the people in the foster care system). We will explore these particular experiences of loss and ambiguity more in Chapter 4 when we explore the question, Who are these people?

By tuning into the experiences of children and the advice that they offer, we can become more aware of how startling and confusing the notification of being placed in foster care can be for a child.

Mark's Experience
13 years old

Mark reflects on what happened when he found out he was moving into foster care. He states, "I got surrounded in my room by these two workers, and I was just like I got really mad. They said that, ah, 'How's everything there?' And I'm like, 'Alright.' And they're like, 'Um, you're not doing so well,' or something, 'so you got to come with us.' I was like, 'Whoa. I don't even know where I'm going. My God, this is like weird and stuff.'"

Sandra's Advice
10 years old

Sandra discusses how being informed about the need to move from her home would have been helpful to her getting ready for foster care. She advises that "[it would have been helpful to] at least be told that I was moving instead of me having to run into my house and cry . . . Like saying, 'Hi, my name is blah, blah, blah' and said, 'You're moving.' Then we would have known and we would probably be OK."

Chana's Advice
20 years old

Chana's reflection on the day she transitioned into foster care echoes the concerns of Mark and Sandra. She shares, "It was really painful the day I had to leave.

As soon as I got off the bus, [the Department of Social Services] and a police-man were there. I was thinking to myself, 'Did somebody kill somebody?' Or you know, 'Did something happen?' As soon as I got in the house, the caseworker told me to pack my things. I was very scared. My sibling and I had just got off the bus, and my baby brother was crying because he didn't want to leave, so it was really a traumatic moment. I really think that someone, my caseworker, she should have told me what was going on exactly. I think that would have been a whole lot help-ful. What was not helpful was that we were in a rush. I was scared because the policeman was there and, you know, they had to write reports and they asked me questions, and it was all so much at one moment and I couldn't bear to under-stand, you know, what was happening." Chana's experience illustrates confusion, fear, trauma, a lack of communication, and questions she had that were not being answered. To mitigate experiences such as these happening to other children in the future, Chana offers the following advice: "My advice to caregivers is to talk to the child that's going through the traumatic situation. Not only just the child, but siblings, you know, siblings could probably help, and I really think that is very important for the caseworker to understand and know." Chana's advice is note-worthy as it highlights children's need for communication when they are being removed from their home, as well as a recognition of people who are significant to the child (in this case, the child's siblings). Children may become distraught when they fear their significant relationships are being threatened, their concerns are not addressed, and their questions are left unanswered.

As these reports illustrate, children often clearly remember the events and/or emo-tions they experienced when they were notified of the need to be placed in foster care. These events and emotions were frequently depicted as stressful experiences

---

HEALING SUGGESTION 1.1
C.A.R.E. FOR CHILDREN'S FOSTER CARE NOTIFICATION

Children's reports suggest that it is important for care providers to be sensitive to how difficult it can be for them when they are removed from their home. If children believe their personal well-being is threatened, feelings of fear, anxiety, sadness, and anger may surface. If possible, an adult with whom the child is familiar should be the one to advise the child of the need to be placed in foster care. If it is not possible for children to be notified by an adult with whom they are familiar, the person who is notifying the child should take the time to introduce himself or herself, should explain who he or she is, and should be sensitive to the child's feelings and interpretations when notify-ing the child of the need to be placed in foster care.

that left a lasting impression throughout their time in foster care. If experiences that have the potential to be stressful to children can be minimized, then a sound argument can be made for the importance of understanding strategies to mitigate the negative effects of these experiences. The first healing suggestion, *C.A.R.E. for Children's Foster Care Notification*, identifies how care providers can create a less stressful experience for children when they are notified that they are being placed in foster care.

WHAT ABOUT MY FAVORITE ...?

Recognizing and acknowledging the personal belongings that are significant to a child can be helpful to children during their transition into foster care. Unfortunately, these belongings, as well as how they can assist children during the transition into foster care, can go unnoticed by adults during this abrupt transaction.

Denise's Experience
13 years old

Denise reports, "I wanted to bring my [musical instrument], like go back into my house and get my [musical instrument], but they didn't let me. They didn't bother asking me [if I wanted to bring it], so I asked, and then they said, 'No, you are not allowed. You can't go back home.' Like, whatever. I was pretty pissed because I really needed my stuff because I had [music] lessons that night, too. I was really mad." What is noteworthy about Denise's experience is that even though she had been removed from her home, she had the intention to maintain her commitment to her music lessons on the very same evening that she had moved to a new residence. This experience also suggests that children may not have a clear understanding of how being placed in foster care has the potential to significantly alter their assumptive world. Denise's experience demonstrates the importance of recognizing and acknowledging a child's commitments, especially during a period of change. Children, like adults, often seek stability and consistency in their lives; especially during moments of traumatic loss events. Because stability and continuity are fundamental to a child's development and well-being (Gilligan, 2001), it is possible that attending to a child's objects of significance (in this case, her musical instrument) could provide something tangible that would contribute to a sense of stability and continuity. It would be hoped that, if possible, efforts would be made not only for Denise to bring her musical instrument but also for her to pursue her music lessons.

Angela's Experience
12 years old

When Angela moved into her new house, "it was like, OK, I don't have any pajamas, don't have nuttin. While we were there we just made a list of what the stuff that we wanted from my mom and, most of it, I haven't got. Like, [my brother got me] a toy, he's my favorite, and I still haven't got him, because my mom apparently can't find him. But if I went into my room, you'd just open the door, and you'd know exactly where it is." The toy given to her by her brother was considered significant to Angela, and she had hoped that she could have it returned to her. As Angela expresses, she believes she could easily retrieve this toy if provided the opportunity. If a care provider invited Angela to speak about this issue, it is likely that Angela would communicate her concerns and ideas about this important toy and, in turn, the care provider could address these concerns. Although the toy might not be able to be retrieved, it is possible that having the opportunity to discuss her concerns with someone would create a relational space where her needs and matters of significance could be validated.

Musical instruments, pets, beds, toys, and jewelry are just a few of the personal belongings that children identify as being important items that were "left behind." As is discussed by Gabriella and Tracey, what is particularly important to note about these items is that they often can serve as meaningful tools for children as they try to cope with loss.

Gabriella's Experience
12 years old

Gabriella reflects on how she felt once she learned she would not be returning to her original home in the near future. She states, "Well, after my social worker told me I wasn't going to go home for a while, then I got mad and upset and stuff and scared . . . I brought my um, there's this [stuffed animal] . . . my parents bought me a chimpanzee, and I brought that with me [and it made me feel better]."

Tracey's Advice
23 years old

Tracey also recalls the importance of a toy given to her by her parent before entering foster care. She shares, "I remember going into a group home where we weren't allowed to have doll babies. And I'm sorry, I'm a big kid. Like I don't have it anymore because they lost it through my transition, but my dad gave me a doll baby for Christmas and that was what I hung on to when I was going through hard times. I remember going into my first group home, and they said we couldn't have anything that could potentially be a harm to other people, and apparently the doll baby's hands and head were made out of something. It wasn't glass or anything, but it was harder than cotton. So I wasn't allowed to have it, and it took forever for them to bend their rules so I could have it when I was going through a hard time." For Tracey, simply having her "doll baby" would have meant the world to her in terms of coping with "hard times." She believes that "it would have been really helpful for them to ask me if it would be OK for them to go get me another stuffed animal or something that could take the place of that. They could have asked, 'Is there something I can get you that can comfort you during this time? Is there something that we can help you with?'" Perhaps a child's toy, doll, or other object of significance cannot be retrieved, but as Tracey advises, there are other options that can be offered. Although offering a replacement toy would not have been her first choice, she would have preferred having a replacement toy than nothing at all.

Often a child's removal from the home may need to occur swiftly due to safety concerns; however, it is helpful to remember that children's personal belongings are valuable to them and, in the absence of these belongings, they may suffer from yet another experience of loss. The second healing suggestion, *C.A.R.E. for Children's Personal Belongings,* discusses ways to consider the inclusion of children's personal belongings during their transfer to the foster care placement.

HEALING SUGGESTION 1.2
C.A.R.E. FOR CHILDREN'S PERSONAL BELONGINGS

Children entering foster care likely have important and meaningful belongings that may be easy to transfer to their new home and that can assist them in coping with loss. When it is safe to do so, children can be asked about the toys, games, and other items of importance that they may like to bring with them. If this option is not available, children could be asked after they are placed in care if there are any belongings that they would like an adult to retrieve on their behalf. Offering children an option to have personal belongings that are meaningful and significant to them not only can assist with providing children with comfort during stressful situations, but also can assist them in having something tangible that connects them to their original family (i.e., the family with whom they resided prior to entering foster care), friends, and life before entering foster care.

WHY DO I HAVE TO LEAVE?

But why? This question rings through children's minds. Although some children may understand why they are in foster care, many do not (Lee & Whiting, 2007; Mitchell, 2008). Perhaps they were not told why they had to go; perhaps they were told a reason but they still don't understand; perhaps they were told a reason but they don't agree with it; or perhaps they were told too many reasons and now they are confused. Having no information, too little information, or too much conflicting information can create confusion and uncertainty for children who are trying to make sense of why they have been placed in foster care and precipitates *placement reason ambiguity* (Mitchell, 2008; Mitchell & Kuczynski, 2010). Placement reason ambiguity occurs when a child has a lack of clarity about the reason for his or her placement in foster care. The following reports illustrate children's experiences of placement reason ambiguity.

Craig's Experience
12 years old

Craig wasn't sure why he entered foster care. He states, "I just left for some reason. I don't really know why."

Derrick's Experience
13 years old

Derrick also reports that he didn't know the reason for being placed in foster care. He explains, "Not even now, they don't even tell me . . . [My worker] doesn't know, and [my lawyer] and them don't even know about it."

Denise's Experience
13 years old

When speaking with Denise, she replies, "Oh, I just moved into my foster house, and I was crying for my mom and stuff." Denise reported that no one told her why she was entering foster care and, after time, she still didn't have an idea why she was placed in foster care because she had now "kind of set it aside."

Sandra's Experience
10 years old

Sandra discussed being upset and confused about being placed in foster care because "I knew that my mom wasn't doing anything wrong." In this case, Sandra was aware of why she had been placed in foster care but experienced a lack of clarity because she did not believe the reason that was given to her.

Angela's Experience
12 years old

Angela discusses how she was advised of the need to be placed in foster care and her confusion about why she was in foster care. She explains, "I whispered to my sisters, like, 'Does anybody know what's going on other than mom and this weirdo. This grouchy weirdo. Like, what's happening?' And then we went into the office, and she sat us in the little glass room and she told us we weren't allowed to live with our mom anymore. Then we kept asking why and she said like 'That's for another time.' . . . Even kids have come up to me and I'll be like 'Guys, help me make some sense out of this!' and they'd be like, 'Sure, I have no friggin idea!' Cause, I've even asked teachers, 'Why do you think I'm in care?' I've had this, this, this, this, this, this, this, like I'm given a million different reasons, and like, don't ask me cause I've got no clue. Nobody really knows, and I'm pretty sure it's all the reasons . . . I'll be like, 'OK you know what my mom said that I lied and that's why I'm in care,' and I was like, 'No way. It's never anything the kids do, it's cause the parents can't pull their head out of their ass. I know that (laughs) 'cause at first when my mom told me that it was my fault, it's like 'You're tripping right?' It's just like, 'Well, you lied and that's why you're here. So it's your own doings.' I was, like, 'Alrighty then.' It's always because of the parents. It's always because the parents don't know how to treat the kids. It's nothing that the kids do.'" Fortunately, Angela was aware that she was in foster care because "her parents didn't know how to treat the kids" and not because of anything she had done. Nonetheless, knowing that she was in foster care for a reason other than her own doing still did not prevent Angela from experiencing placement reason ambiguity because she did not know *why* she was in foster care.

It is not uncommon for children in foster care to create their own interpretations of why they have been placed in foster care (Mitchell, 2008; Palmer, 1996; Unrau et al., 2008; Whiting & Lee, 2003). For example, Dominick (9 years old) asserted, "The reason we moved into foster care is because me and my brother used to run away from school because we thought it was boring." Although Dominick appears to have "clarity" about his foster care placement, this example demonstrates the need for communication with children about the reason for their placement in foster care.

False interpretations can negatively affect children's psychological well-being (Auden, 1995; Piaget, 1930). If children are not provided with a reason for their placement in foster care and have this reason revisited throughout their time in care, it is quite possible that these children will believe that they are to blame or some other erroneous attribution. Self-blame can lead to feelings of guilt, and guilt often precipitates low self-esteem (DeSpelder & Strickland, 2010). The belief that they are to blame for their placement in foster care could be detrimental not only to their own well-being, but also to the development of healthy relationships within new family units.

The third healing suggestion, *C.A.R.E. for Children's Experiences of Placement Reason Ambiguity*, discusses healthier ways for children to understand and make sense of the reason for being placed in foster care, thus minimizing placement reason ambiguity.

HEALING SUGGESTION 1.3
C.A.R.E. FOR CHILDREN'S EXPERIENCES OF PLACEMENT
REASON AMBIGUITY

A false sense of reality can create chaos and confusion. It is not helpful to convey untruthful or fabricated reasons for why a child has been placed in foster care. Although someone may have good intentions, it is harmful to children to receive information that is dishonest. Any information that is shared with children should always be based on the truth of the situation and should be shared with them in an age-appropriate manner.

Providing children with a clear and concise reason for why they are in foster care can help them to develop healthier interpretations about why they are being removed from their families. Care providers can assist children by providing them with age-appropriate explanations while being sensitive to their understanding and interpretations. Similar to other explanations of loss (DeSpelder & Strickland, 2010), the reason for placement in foster care should be simple and based on facts. Invite children to ask questions and provide them with honest and child-appropriate answers.

Most important, children need to know that the reason for placement in foster care has nothing to do with them. *It is not their fault!* Reminding children of this fact will assist them in their healing of loss and grief. Because children will evaluate and re-evaluate this information over time, it is essential to reconnect with them to help guide their understanding in a safe and honest direction (Eagle, 1994).

CAN MY MOM OR DAD COME WITH ME?

When children learn that they must move from their home, they may ask if their parent(s) can come with them. Because children often don't know, understand, or agree with *why* they are being placed in foster care, they may also be confused about why their parent(s) are not able to come with them. While some children, such as Brenda, have reported that having their parent accompany them would create additional stress for them, others, like Sandra, have expressed that they would have liked their parent to be with them as they were relocated to a new home.

Brenda's Experience
11 years old

Brenda states that she wouldn't want her mom to accompany her to the foster home because "then I'd get more attached to my real mom and then it'd be harder to let go when she has to go home." We hear Brenda's concern about having to say goodbye to her "real mom" when entering foster care. For Brenda, having her mom present (if it was possible) would not have been helpful to her because of how difficult it would be to say goodbye.

Sandra's Experience
10 years old

Sandra, on the hand, shares how she would have preferred to have her mom with her when she moved to her foster home. Sandra first shares that her mother told her that "all of us were going to an appointment . . . Then when she told me the truth, she said, 'I'm not going.' . . . I would have liked her to go and see my home and check it out, but she didn't." When entering foster care, Sandra was under the impression that she was "going to an appointment" and that her mother would be accompanying her. She soon discovered that neither of these statements was true.

The fourth healing suggestion, *C.A.R.E. for Children's Preference for Parental Accompaniment*, addresses how care providers can attend to children's feelings about having their parent present during the transition to the foster care placement.

HEALING SUGGESTION 1.4
C.A.R.E. FOR CHILDREN'S PREFERENCE FOR PARENTAL
ACCOMPANIMENT

Some children may prefer having their parent present when they are being placed in foster care, whereas others may not. If it is safe, in the best interest of the child, and the child's preference, a parent could be invited to accompany the child to his or her first placement. This could provide a sense of security and comfort for children during the transition. In many cases it is neither safe nor in the best interest of children to have their parent accompany them to the placement. In situations such as these, it may be helpful to determine if there is a personal belonging that was given to children by their parents or reminds them of their parent that could accompany them as they transition into foster care (see Healing Suggestion 1.2).

CAN I HAVE SOME TIME TO SAY GOODBYE TO MY FAMILY?

It can be scary for children when they are told that their life is about to change drastically, especially when their parents and maybe even siblings will not be there with them during this time. Children report feelings of fear and anxiety about being removed from their loved ones and how having additional information and a processing period could assist them during this time.

Mark's Advice
13 years old

Mark offers the following advice to care providers who are removing a child from their original home, "Say, 'Do you want some time to grab your stuff? You are going to come with me, say goodbye to everyone.' And don't rush them . . . Getting rushed out makes you like mad because you are already bad, trying to keep up . . . Depends what kind of kid you get, too . . . Like if you get someone who's like, I don't know, if they're like, if they don't like it at their house. They're like, 'I need out of here,' then you can do that stuff. They're not going to be mad but you get someone who's sitting there, and they look like they want to freak and they know what is going on, then try not to say too much. Like be easy on them. Don't be rushing them like they were with me. That got me like right, Oh!" Mark discusses the importance of being asked about his personal belongings and having an opportunity to say goodbye to his family. Reflecting on his experience, Mark shares how being notified of having to be removed from his home and family caused him upset and confusion. He also mentions how it is important to consider the child's personality and situation, as each child may experience the removal from his or her home differently; however, as will be discussed in the next section, most children express reluctance to be removed from their homes.

Alicja's Advice
14 years old

Similar to Mark, Alicja suggests that children should have time with their family to process their need to be placed in foster care. She also discusses the importance of helping children understand the reason for their placement in care—that is, the way to assist children who are experiencing placement reason ambiguity. She offers the following advice to care providers who are helping a youth get ready to enter a new home, "You could like talk to like the whole family and say the reason why and be like 'This is the reason why we're taking you to foster care, and you will be going to court or whatever, and your parents will try to get you back, and we'll try and help to get you guys back but this is a job for us, and it depends on the court what happens.' And I don' t know, like tell them like the reason and everything and try to make it they know the reason and take them out for a drink or something and let them spend time with their family for a little bit before they go. Let them go somewhere with the family for a day and then take them the next day and let them hug and kiss and talk and still say that they'll still be able to see each other but as long as it's supervised or depends on what it is. Um, they could ask the child, 'Are [you] upset about what's going on?' And if they are, then say, 'Why?' and like the kid will answer and then try to fix it and say, 'Well, we don't really want to do this but this is our job, and we could probably try to get you to go back with your family. Depends on the court or whatever it is. Hopefully you can get back with your family but if not, we're hoping that you get along with your foster parents.'" Alicja's advice echoes the value of communicating with children about their need to be placed in foster care and for providing thoughtful and honest information about the foster care system. She also highlights how care providers can recognize and acknowledge the fears children have about being separated from their families, affirming their worthiness of unconditional love during times of stress and trauma, and explaining how their relationships with their family and new care providers will be attended to.

The fifth healing suggestion, *C.A.R.E. for Family Processing Time*, addresses the opportunity for children to have processing time with their families once they have been notified of the need to be placed in foster care.

HEALING SUGGESTION 1.5
C.A.R.E. FOR FAMILY PROCESSING TIME

Providing children time to spend with their families so they can process the need to be placed in foster care may be helpful to children in multiple ways. This time could be used by children to collect important, meaningful belongings and to speak to their families about any concerns and/or fears they may have. The length of family processing time (e.g., a couple of hours, an overnight discussion, or a couple of days) would be dependent on each child's specific situation and needs. With the proper guidance and assistance, family processing time could be used to better support children's mental and physical preparation for their impending "temporary" placement in a new home.

DO I HAVE TO LEAVE?

Let's revisit the earlier scenario in which you were asked to contemplate coming home from an ordinary day to find your bags packed and were told that you had to leave your family immediately. Can you recall a time in your life when you lost something or someone you loved without any notice? How did that feel? Did you feel despair, confusion, sadness, or anger? Taking these feelings into consideration, then, one can likely understand why many children are resistant to being removed from their homes. As illustrated in the experiences of Jessica, Henry, and Derrick, this resistance can present itself in many ways, from reluctant adherence to outright refusal.

Jessica's Experience
12 years old

Jessica recalls when she received the news that she would be leaving her home, "I walked in the door, and I'm like 'Mom, what's going on?' and she's like, 'You're going,' and I'm like 'Why?' and she said, 'Cause last night,' and I'm like 'Oh.' And yeah we started getting our things, and she's like 'Bye' . . . I was sad about leaving my mom and the stuff behind that I really like."

Henry's Experience
8 years old

Henry discusses how he resisted attempts by strangers who were trying to get him in their car. He shares, "They had a hard time putting me in the car . . . I was playing with my friends [outside, away from my home]. They were calling my name, but I was ignoring them [I didn't know who they were]. They came out of the car, and then I just ran somewhere . . . and then finally they got me in." Henry's experience illustrates how some children may feel threatened by adults, who are complete strangers, attempt to "put [them] in the car." Many children are taught at a young age not to get into a car with strangers. One can only imagine how Henry felt when strangers were calling his name and trying to force him into their car. Although the "strangers" were adults who were authorized to protect and care for Henry, it can be helpful for care providers to consider how this event can be interpreted and experienced by an 8-year-old child.

Derrick's Experience
13 years old

Derrick also discusses his outright reluctance to be removed from his home, "Yeah, I wouldn't go, and the worker said that they were going to call the cops and then I'd wait until they called and I waited until they were on their way and I left." It was not until the police were called and Derrick realized that they were on his way to his home that he decided to leave with the worker.

As these reports demonstrate, fears can heighten for children when they are being removed from their home: the fear of loss, the fear of change, the fear of ambiguity, the fear of what lies ahead. Although many of these children must be temporarily removed from their homes and families for their own safety, the fact that children are terrified of this abrupt change should not be overlooked. Mark advises how care providers can be sensitive to children's feelings during this tumultuous time.

Mark's Advice
13 years old

Mark states, "Like if they're sitting there freaking out, try to get them to cool down before they go and all this stuff because if they get in the car and they're losing it, they're going to be a lot worse when they get near that car." To get them to cool down, care providers could "talk to them" but "it depends what they were saying. Like, 'It's not bad. You're just going to a foster home.' That's like when I would have lost it . . . It's like, how about me and you trade lives for a bit and you can see what it's like . . . You could like even get like a person who has been in a foster home and say like, 'I've done this and stuff. It's not as bad as you think in the end. It's alright. You are allowed to go and make your own choices and do this, do that. It will work out fine.'" Mark expresses the importance of communicating with children in a way that is respectful and compassionate. His advice also lends itself to potential policy and program enhancements that could involve having individuals with foster care experience present with the child during the removal from the home and transfer to their foster care placement.

In the sixth healing suggestion, *C.A.R.E. for Children's Experiences of the Home Transfer*, we reflect on how compassion and social support are necessary travel companions for children as they transition out of their homes and into foster care.

HEALING SUGGESTION 1.6
C.A.R.E. FOR CHILDREN'S EXPERIENCES OF THE HOME TRANSFER

During the relocation to a new home, children need to be in the presence of adults who are supportive, understanding, and considerate of their feelings. It is important to acknowledge that children are struggling with a multitude of emotions during this time and are likely juggling loss, confusion, and ambiguity simultaneously. Care providers are encouraged to communicate compassionately while recognizing and acknowledging how they are feeling and being sensitive to what they are experiencing.

In situations where police officers are present during a child's removal from his or her home, it is especially important for children to know that they have not done anything wrong and that the police officers are there to support them and not to "punish" them. Because the police uniform can be intimidating and scary for many children, it may be helpful to children if police officers, when possible, arrive at the child's home in citizen's attire rather than in uniform. This may be especially helpful in jurisdictions where the police are responsible for removing children from their homes. Ultimately, during the critical, and potentially traumatic, period of being notified of the need to be removed from one's home and the actual removal from one's home, it is important for children to be notified and accompanied by adults who are trained in child-centered foster care transfers and, preferably, adults who have child welfare experience. In addition, if there is a youth advocate who has been assigned by the child welfare agency to assist with the relocation of children to child welfare residences, invite him or her to be present during this time. Remember that some children will want to talk, whereas others will not. Each child is unique, and his or her specific personality and needs should be considered and respected during the relocation to a new residence.

FROM THE WHY TO THE WHAT?

"It happens so quick and you're just gone and like see you later."
MARK, 13 years old

Without much preparation, children are notified of the need to be removed from their homes and their families, often without a clear understanding of why this is all happening in the first place. Filled with confusion, anxiety, and fear, children are told they need to leave their families and homes because they are going into "foster care." A child's removal often happens quickly with little to no time to collect their personal belongings, process what is happening, or say a personal goodbye to their families. Bags in hand, children are forced to venture into the unknown, trusting unfamiliar adults and uncharted territories. Their minds fill with questions, awaiting answers.

Why do I have to leave?
WHAT IS FOSTER CARE?
Where are you taking me?
Who are these people?

How about me?
When can I go home?

Hearts beat fast. Everything has happened so quickly! Hurry up and get in the car—it's on its way to our next stop. Our journey of loss, ambiguity, C.A.R.E., and healing continues.

"I didn't even know the meaning back then . . . I felt it was kinda like prison 'cause I went into a locked area. There was a locked door. Everything was locked. I was like, Is this prison? Am I in trouble? Am I going to jail?"
BRENDA, 11 years old

2

WHAT Is Foster Care?

AS THE CAR drives away, we hear a child whisper from the backseat, "What exactly *is* foster care?" This "what" question surfaces in children's minds as they are removed from their homes and placed in the foster care system. Although many children may not understand the meaning of foster care, they quickly discover that, whatever its meaning, it does involve a significant change in their lives.

Children who have had no previous experience with the foster care system may have heard the phrase "foster care"; however, it is likely that many, if not most, of these children are unfamiliar with the meaning of foster care. What is it? What does it mean to be *in* foster care? What does foster care entail? It is not uncommon for children to be unsure of the rules and expectations within the foster care system (Bruskas, 2008; Mitchell & Kuczynski, 2010; Unrau et al., 2008). Some of the questions that may run through a child's mind include, but are not limited to, What will happen to me? Will I ever see my family again? What is going to happen to my parents? Will I be fed? Do I have to change schools? . . . and the list goes on.

Take a moment to situate this childhood experience within an adult context. Imagine you arrive home one day to unexpectedly receive a court order that states you must leave the premises immediately. Included in the proviso is the notification that you will be losing your home and your primary means of transportation, will be separated from your family, and will be placed in a system referred to as "foster care." Perhaps similar questions would enter your mind: What or from whom do I need protection? Where are my spouse or children going to live? How will I get to work? What is going to happen to me? Referring back now to a child's experience, consider how this situation could affect a child who is in a much less developmentally and cognitively privileged position than most adults. In this chapter, I will explain how *structural ambiguity* (i.e., a lack of clarity about the meaning and implicit and explicit rules of the foster care system; Mitchell, 2008; Mitchell & Kuczynski, 2010) can affect how a child enters, perceives, and engages with the foster care system.

WHAT IS THE MEANING OF FOSTER CARE?

Although some adults may assume that children understand the concept of foster care, children's reports suggest that many are unaware of the meaning of foster care at the time of entry.

Sandra's Experience
10 years old

Sandra recalls the question she raised when she was told she was going into foster care. She asked, "Mom, why is there people packing our stuff?" And she said, "You are going into foster care." I said, "What is that?" She's like, "Where people take care of you, cause I can't."

Deborah's Experience
15 years old

"[When I moved to my new home] I was scared because I was going into foster care." When asked if she knew the definition of foster care, Deborah replies, "No," and that no one told her. She didn't talk to anyone about why she was scared, including her siblings. This example demonstrates how some children will not openly discuss their fears about foster care when entering the foster care system. Children may not communicate their fears because they are overwhelmed with emotion, they don't trust the strangers whom they are with, or they may find it difficult formulating their questions. It is important for adults not to wait for children to ask questions; rather, all children should be provided with an orientation to the foster care system (Bruskas, 2008). Ensuring that children's questions and experiences of structural ambiguity are attended to could mitigate some of the fears, anxiety, and trauma they experience when entering the foster care system.

Craig's Advice
12 years old

When asked how a case manager might be able to assist children during their transition to a new home, Craig suggests that case managers "tell [children] where you're going and ask them what they need know and whatever they need to know, you should tell them." Craig's advice highlights the importance of children having an understanding of "where they are going" (i.e., foster care), asking children questions about their concerns, and providing them with answers they are seeking.

Unfortunately, children continue to struggle with understanding the meaning of foster care well after placement. When children who, on average, had been in care for a year and a half were asked if they understood the meaning of foster care, many replied, "I don't know." It is disconcerting that there are children who have been removed from their homes for more than a year and still do not have an understanding about the system in which they have been placed. Once removed from their home, children would benefit from an understanding of the system that is meant to care for them and the ways in which their needs will be met.

HEALING SUGGESTION 2.1
C.A.R.E. FOR CHILDREN'S EXPERIENCES OF STRUCTURAL AMBIGUITY

Children should be provided with information about the foster care system to help ease the anxiety or stress that may occur as a result of a lack of clarity about the system designed to care for them. Other researchers have also emphasized the importance of providing children with information to help them understand the purpose of foster care (Bruskas, 2008). Although understanding the intention of foster care will not ease all of children's anxieties associated with removal from their families, this information may be helpful in minimizing unhealthy conclusions drawn by children's active imaginations. Care providers can advise children that child welfare residences (e.g., foster homes, group homes, etc.) are a safe and welcoming place for children to live while they are placed away from their original homes. Unless this is not the case for a specific child, all children should be advised, immediately upon the removal from their homes, that they *will* see their families again, that foster care is not intended to be a long-term experience, and that efforts will be made to reunite them with their family when their family environment is safe for them to return.

AM I GOING TO PRISON?

In the absence of understanding the implicit and explicit rules of the foster care system, children's imaginations can become overactive in a way that proves to be harmful to their perceptions of the system designed to care for and protect them.

Brenda's Experience
11 years old

Brenda states, "I felt it was like, kinda like prison 'cause I went into a locked area. There was a locked door. Everything was locked. I was like, 'Is this prison? Am I in trouble? Am I going to jail?" Brenda's initial experience of the child welfare agency implies a fearful perception of the foster care system. Institutions and agencies can seem cold and sterile, to children and adults alike. Some children are brought to a child welfare agency or another institution before arriving at their foster care placement and, as Brenda's experience illustrates, these institutions can heighten their fears. Unfortunately, without the necessary communication, these children may believe that this "first stop" is their new home.

HEALING SUGGESTION 2.2
C.A.R.E. FOR CHILDREN'S EXPERIENCES OF THE PLACEMENT
ROUTE AND PROCESS

Because children are often unaware of where they are going and where they will
be living after immediate removal from their home, children may draw assumptions about any intermediate locations where they arrive prior to the foster care
placement. Although care providers are aware that the intermediate location is
not the child's new place of residence, this may not be apparent to the child. In
turn, children may find it helpful to be notified of any "location stops" that they
may encounter before arriving at their residential placement, especially if it is an
institution or agency, and being advised that this location is *not* where they will
be residing.

WHAT WILL HAPPEN TO MY RELATIONSHIPS
ONCE I AM IN FOSTER CARE?

When placed in foster care, children begin to question how their familial relationships will be affected and are often uncertain about how they will be cared for, how
their lives will change, and if they will ever see their loved ones again.

Brenda's Experience
11 years old

Brenda states, "Well, I thought when I first went into foster care that
I wouldn't be able to see my parents ever again . . . Even though my parents
didn't do right, they weren't right to me, they weren't being right ah with
me . . . it doesn't mean I don't like them. But, like, it kinda feels like prison
if you didn't get to see them." The thought of being permanently separated
from one's family can be considered by children as unfair, unjustified, and
confusing.

Odelia's Experience
12 years old

Odelia states, "I was afraid that I'd never get to see my mom again, and I was
afraid that I wouldn't get to see my sister except for at school . . . and, I was
kind of afraid too, that, um, they wouldn't let me live back with my mom. Like,
ever move back with her."

HEALING SUGGESTION 2.3
C.A.R.E. FOR CHILDREN'S EXPERIENCES OF FAMILY THREAT

Children may feel threatened by the foster care system if they believe it is the reason for their separation from loved ones (e.g., parents, siblings, and friends). Feeling threatened can elicit discomfort, anxiety, and depression. To help mitigate feelings of threat or hostility, care providers can take the time to explain to children how the significant relationships in their lives will be maintained after they have been placed in foster care. Communicating with children and asking them which relationships are important to them can be a first step in identifying the relationships they consider significant. Once these relationships have been identified, advising children about the efforts that will be made to maintain these significant relationships can be helpful in building a relational home. Furthermore, providing children with an understanding of how their relationships will be maintained may help to alleviate any potentially hostile feelings that children may have toward a system that is intended to protect and care for them.

WILL I BE TAKEN CARE OF WHEN I AM IN FOSTER CARE?

Will I be fed? Will I have clothes? Will I have a place to sleep? Questions about whether their basic needs will be met in foster care may enter children's minds without ever being vocalized. As was demonstrated earlier with Deborah's experience, it is not uncommon for children to keep their fears to themselves. When these questions are left unacknowledged or unaddressed, children may ruminate about fears of the unknown. The importance of providing contextual information to answer these specific questions will be elaborated on in the next chapter when *placement context ambiguity* is discussed; however, it is helpful to consider how providing children with answers to these questions from the onset can be helpful in alleviating unnecessary fears.

Miguel's Advice
8 years old

When asked what caseworkers should take into consideration when placing a child in foster care, Miguel emphasizes the importance of ensuring that children's basic needs are met. He advises, "Make sure the child is fed, has clothes, a hat, pants, and a room." It would naturally follow that this information would be communicated as well as demonstrated to the child.

Sandra's Advice
10 years old

Children may also question whether there will be anyone with whom they can speak about their concerns and fears. Sandra offers the following advice to children entering foster care, "You're gonna get a worker and um, ask your worker for a counselor, and you can tell a counselor how you really feel." Sandra's advice illustrates that it is beneficial for children in foster care to have a case manager *and* a counselor. She advises children to advocate for themselves and ask their case manager for a counselor because you can tell the counselor "how you *really* feel." Supporting this advice, it is important for children to have multiple adults in their lives with whom they can speak and openly express their emotions.

HEALING SUGGESTION 2.4
C.A.R.E. FOR CHILDREN'S BASIC NEEDS

Children may or may not openly communicate their fears about whether their basic needs will be met. Care providers can assist children by asking them about their fears, acknowledging their fears as important, and assuring children that they will be fed, clothed, housed, and cared for while in foster care. By providing an explanation of how a child's needs will be met and the adult's specific role in meeting these needs (caseworkers and parental caregivers have different roles and these should be identified to the child), a child's stressful feelings and experiences may be minimized. If and whenever possible, children should be given the opportunity and encouraged to speak with a counselor or therapist at the onset and throughout their placement in the foster care system.

DO I NEED TO CHANGE SCHOOLS?

Although federal laws such as the McKinney-Vento Act in the United States encourage and support the educational stability of youth in foster care (Chambers & Palmer, 2011), the unfortunate reality is that being placed in foster care can generate the need for children to relocate to new schools. It is not uncommon for children in foster care to be placed outside their community (Blome, 1997) and to experience educational challenges (Bruskas, 2008) and multiple school changes while in the foster care system (Casey Family Programs, 2007).

Denise's Experience
13 years old

Denise recalls the frequency and impact of school changes when she entered foster care, "Yep, three different schools in one year . . . When I found out that

I was moving from my school I was bawling my eyes out for at least a week."
As Denise's report illustrates, the need to change schools can be a recurring
experience for children in foster care and one that can stir up feelings of sadness and loss.

Brenda's Experience
11 years old

Brenda states, "[Changing schools when I moved] was kind of hard because
like all the people that I knew. It felt like I was moving like again 'cause like
even though I stayed in the same spot and just transferred schools, it just felt
like I was moving again, like you were leaving everybody behind." Although
Brenda "stayed in the same spot," she discusses how transferring schools was
stressful to her because she lost important relational connections. A change
in school placement during one's time in foster care can elicit feelings of loss
similar to those that are experienced by children when they are moved to a
new home. In Chapter 6, we will delve further into children's loss experiences
and ways children cope with *ambiguous loss* (i.e., a lack of clarity about the
psychological or physical presence of members in their psychological family;
Boss, 1999).

HEALING SUGGESTION 2.5
C.A.R.E. FOR CHILDREN'S EXPERIENCES OF SCHOOL THREAT

Not all children who are placed in foster care will be required to change schools; however, some children will be faced with this experience. It may be helpful to children if
care providers notify them *if* the need to change schools is necessary (or is not necessary) and the rationale for this decision. If children are required to change schools,
care providers could potentially mitigate additional trauma by helping children maintain their significant relationships. When possible, scheduling weekend visits or after-
school study groups with friends from their original school or supporting continued
extracurricular activities with these friends may be helpful to children during their
transition to a new school. Other options may include written, electronic, or tele-
phone correspondence, weekend outings, or summer leisure activities.

WHAT ARE SOME OF THE GOOD THINGS ABOUT FOSTER CARE?

Children entering foster care for the first time may experience stress and fear due to
this new change in their lives and being unclear about the meaning of this change.

As was illustrated in Deborah's experience earlier in the chapter, children who experience structural ambiguity may choose to internalize their emotions instead of talk about them. Brenda and Mark suggest that children's fear of the "unknowns" of foster care may be somewhat alleviated if the positive elements of foster care are shared with them as they transition into the foster care system.

Brenda's Advice
11 years old

Brenda offers the following advice to care providers, "Tell them a lot of good stuff about foster care and tell them they won't regret this and all that."

Mark's Advice
13 years old

Mark suggests that children may appreciate learning about the benefits of being in foster care. He advises that telling children, "It's not as bad as you think in the end. It's alright. You are allowed to go and make your own choices and do this, do that. It will work out fine," can be encouraging and helpful to children entering foster care.

HEALING SUGGESTION 2.6
C.A.R.E. FOR CHILDREN'S EXPERIENCES OF FOSTER CARE BENEFITS

Foster care is a system intended to care for children who have experienced abuse or neglect. Children entering foster care are often dealing with multiple traumas. Additional fears or stressors can hinder a child's ability to adapt to a new environment and new relationships. Communicating the benefits of foster care (e.g., a safe home, agency supports and programs, etc.) to children may provide them with a greater sense of comfort and security. This approach may also set a foundation whereby children may be more open to new relationships and engaging in new family environments.

FROM THE WHAT TO THE WHERE?

"Why am I here again? I don't like this place."
BRENDA, 11 years old

As children are transferred from their original homes to their foster care placement, questions race through their minds. Some children experience confusion about the meaning of foster care, fear about whether they have done something wrong and are going to jail, if they will ever see their loved ones again, whether they will be taken care of, if they will need to change schools, and if there is anything good at all about what is transpiring in that very moment. Many children will appraise entering foster care as a threat to their personal well-being and the significant relationships in their lives. This stress appraisal can result in feelings of discomfort, anxiety, and depression. Unfortunately, if not attended to properly, these feelings may become overwhelming to a child and affect his or her ability to effectively cope with other stressors. Children's reports demonstrated that structural ambiguity led to stressful appraisals and, as will be demonstrated in the next chapter, children became further stressed when they experienced placement context ambiguity (i.e., a lack of clarity about the context of the foster home). Unfortunately, children's experiences of psychological stress and trauma often go unspoken and unnoticed during this relatively short, yet critical, removal and placement period. As adults discuss the logistics of the foster care placement, children await clarification and reassurance about the ambiguous experiences that leave them questioning, frightened, and confused.

Why do I have to leave?
What is foster care?
WHERE ARE YOU TAKING ME?
Who are these people?
How about me?
When can I go home?

"I didn't know where I was going to sleep."
JESSICA, 12 years old

3

WHERE Are You Taking Me?

CHILDREN WHO ENTER into non-kinship foster care are most often placed in a foster home or children's home (also known as a group home) with individuals with whom the children are unfamiliar. Depending on the type of placement, children may be moved to a home placement that differs greatly from the structure, environment, and dynamic of their original home. For example, the new placement may have multiple children or no children, pets or no pets, and private or shared bedrooms. Unfortunately, children are often placed in a home knowing little to nothing about the residences where they will be living (Sinclair et al., 2005; Unrau et al., 2008). This lack of information can elicit *placement context ambiguity*—that is, a lack of clarity about the context of the home where they will be residing (Mitchell, 2008; Mitchell & Kuczynski, 2010). In this chapter we will explore some of the common concerns and fears expressed by children who experience placement context ambiguity.

WHO LIVES AT THE HOME?

Moving to a new residence can be a stressful experience for anyone. Children and adults alike are known to be resistant to change. Change, particularly change due to losses, can evoke stress, anxiety, depression, and rumination (Nolen-Hoeksema, Parker, & Larson, 1994). In addition to the need to physically move to a new residence, children in foster care are also confronted with the requirement of living in a new environment with new rules, new people, and new dynamics. Many fears can arise for children when they are unclear about and unprepared for their new living arrangement. These fears could include concerns about who lives in the home, including if any other children will be residing there, and if any pets are present in the home.

Cory's Experience
8 years old

Cory discusses his fears about moving to a new home and familiarizing himself with new people. He states, "I was scared that I wouldn't know the people's house, and it would be more frustrating to get to know them."

Mark's Experience
13 years old

Mark's concerns related to whether he would be the only child in the home. He states, "The only thing that I was like scared to death about is there better be another kid there. So then I could like, I don't know. It would be weird to be alone, like there would just be parents living there and I don't even know them. OK, that's really weird."

Gabriella's Experience
12 years old

Gabriella also expressed her concerns about whether other children would be living in the home; however, unlike Mark, Gabriella expresses that she would prefer to be the only child in the home. She states, "My [caseworker] asked me who I'd like to be with, if there's any kids there or something like that, and how the parents will be. I was like make the parents young and no kids so I can get all the attention."

As these reports illustrate, children often want to know who will be living in their new home. Some children, like Mark, are interested in knowing whether other children will be residing in the home because the thought of being the only child in the home can be frightening; other children, like Gabriella, may want to know if other children live at the home because having other children in the home could be a threat to the personal attention they will receive from their caregivers. In addition to wanting to know if other children reside in the home, many children discussed wanting information about their new home and caregivers prior to the arrival to their placement.

Odelia's Advice
12 years old

Odelia advises that case managers should tell children about the people who are living at the foster care placement. She states, "Well I'm sure that [the case manager] knows the foster parents so [the case manager] could tell [the children] all the great things about the foster parents and just let [the children] know what kind of people [the foster parents] are, and what [the foster parents] expect from [them], and what [the foster parents] don't really mind if you do this or do that—and just tell [the children] if they have any animals or anything, and stuff." Odelia's advice includes sharing information about the care providers, their expectations, and if other people are living at the home.

Angela's Advice
12 years old

Angela discusses the importance of communicating with the children about who they are going to be living with prior to being placed in the home. She advises, "Nobody really filled me in on the way, so, I think it would be good if a kid had their worker or someone to drive them so they can fill them in, so that way, they won't be like, OK, well, what's this lady like and you know, like give them a little piece of paper, what [your caregiver] is like, and that kind of thing."

HEALING SUGGESTION 3.1
C.A.R.E. FOR CHILDREN'S EXPERIENCES OF PLACEMENT
CONTEXT AMBIGUITY

Being placed in a new family environment can be stressful for children. Some may even consider it a traumatic experience. Not knowing where you are going or with whom you are going to be living can be confusing, frustrating, and anxiety provoking. To assist in alleviating placement context ambiguity and structural ambiguity, children could be provided with a care entry information package. This package could include information about the meaning of foster care, how children's basic needs will be met, if other children and/or pets reside in the home, and information about the people (i.e., adults and children) living in the home. Unfortunately, many children are placed in foster care without much forewarning or preparation. It is not uncommon for the adults who are placing the child to have not yet determined the home where the child will be placed upon removing a child from his or her home. As a result, it may not always be possible to provide children with an information package that explains the members who are living in their new home. In situations such as these, it may be helpful to children if they are provided with as much information as possible as it becomes available. Acknowledging and assisting children with their concerns and anxieties during the home transfer can minimize stressful appraisals that could otherwise be circumvented and can provide children with a source of comfort and support.

ARE THERE PETS IN THE HOME?

Questioning whether other children live in the home may not be the only information that children are seeking about their new home; children may also be interested in knowing whether pets live at the home. In the examples that follow, children discuss how pets in the family home can be distinctly considered as friends or foes.

Craig's Experience
12 years old

Craig reports that he "kind of" remembers when he first moved to his foster care placement. "It was scary because of the dogs. As soon as I walked in they started barking and jumping up on me so I thought they were attacking me or something so I screamed and ran out the door and closed the door behind me. Then [my foster mother] took them inside and brought them downstairs and put them in their dog crates. Not like crates that they had to be shipped or something. And then she told me it would be fine and she told me they don't bite and stuff so that was a good relief 'cause I was really scared." Unfortunately, no one communicated to Craig that dogs lived at the home. This situation may have been circumvented if he had been provided with an opportunity to discuss this information with a care provider prior to arriving at the home.

Miguel's Experience
8 years old

Miguel also mentions that when he first moved to his foster home, "there was only a dog that I was scared of." He shared that he did not really like having the animals in the house not because he didn't like them but that "it's just that I'm allergic to some." Because there were many pets in the home, Miguel struggled with his allergies.

Angela's Experience
12 years old

When Angela is asked if there was anyone or anything that was helpful to her when she entered foster care, she replies, "Definitely [my foster mother's] dog and her cat. He'd come and sleep with me 'cause whenever there were new kids in he'd come and sleep with them and ah, [my foster mother] just said that he usually sleeps with the littler ones. So, I was like an exception so it's 'I just got a new best friend, I'm not letting you go!'" As Angela's experience demonstrates, not all children will be fearful of pets. In fact, some children may consider them their "best friend."

These reports illustrate that the presence of pets in a home can be appraised by children as a positive or negative experience. Some children, as illustrated in the experiences of Craig and Miguel, will perceive pets as a threat to their well-being, whereas other children, like Angela, may perceive pets as offering a significant relationship that helps them to cope with the transition into their new home.

In this chapter we have considered how placement context ambiguity includes a lack of clarity about the residents in a child's new home, eliciting questions about the presence of other children and pets. These experiences are primarily elicited *before* children arrive at their foster care placements; however, experiences of placement context ambiguity continue to be experienced once children have arrived at their placements. In the next section, we will explore some of the questions that can arise for children about their new placement in the first few hours and days of their initial placement.

HEALING SUGGESTION 3.2
C.A.R.E. FOR CHILDREN'S PREFERENCES FOR PETS

Before placing a child in a foster care placement, it may be beneficial to ask children whether they like or are allergic to pets before assigning their foster care placement. In some cases, such as emergency removals, a child's preference for or against pets in the home may not be able to be taken into account when deciding on the child's placement; however, it could be helpful to children if their preferences are taken into consideration when it is possible to do so.

Regardless of whether a child's preference for or against pets in the home can be taken into account when deciding on the child's placement, it is important for a child's feelings about pets in the home to be acknowledged and considered when placing a child in a home with pets. Children who have a fear of pets may experience trauma if they are placed in a home with pets without any adult support or assurance. Adults who are placing children in the home can assist children by asking them about their feelings about pets and, if fearful, speaking to the caregivers of the home and requesting some assistance in easing the children into their new surroundings. As Sandra (age 10) advised, "If the home has a dog or cat, you might want to let them know before they come into their house."

WHAT'S BEHIND THAT DOOR?

Children who have experienced traumatic stress naturally may question their new home environment. In addition to wanting to have a good understanding of who lives in the home, children also want to be knowledgeable about the structure of their home. They may have questions about how to find an adult in the middle of the night if they are afraid, where the kitchen is if they are hungry, and whose room not to enter in case the "bogeyman" lives there. The latter example could be read with jest; however, spaces and rooms that are "unaccounted for" may inspire overactive imaginations to develop unhealthy fabricated interpretations that can result in stressful appraisals. Providing children with an opportunity to become acquainted with their surroundings could help to alleviate potential anxiety and ambiguous interpretations of the safety of their home environment.

Denise's Advice
13 years old

Denise offers care providers advice about what they can do to welcome children into their home. She states, "Welcome them in. Also, show them where they're going to be for a while, like where they're going to sleep, where's the washroom."

HEALING SUGGESTION 3.3
C.A.R.E. FOR CHILDREN'S EXPERIENCES OF THEIR HOME ENVIRONMENT

Providing children with a tour of the home where they will be residing is an important first step in welcoming them to and familiarizing them with their new home. Caregivers can introduce children to the spaces and functions of the spaces in the home: the kitchen, the restroom, the laundry room, the bedrooms, the family room, and so on. Familiarizing children with the rooms in the house can minimize potential anxiety about whether their new living environment has the capacity to meet their basic needs. The presence of a kitchen in the home affirms there is a space to store and prepare food, the presence of a restroom affirms there is a space to bathe and attend to personal hygiene, a laundry room affirms there is a space where clothes and linens can be washed, a bedroom affirms there is a place to rest and sleep, and a family room affirms there is a place for the family to gather and spend time together.

During the tour, caregivers can share other relevant information with children about the specific rooms in the house. For example, while in the kitchen, children can be advised, as appropriate, where different foods are located. This information may be particularly helpful to children who are of the age where they can prepare their own meals such as a sandwich or bowl of cereal. When touring the bedrooms of the home, children may also appreciate being advised which room will be theirs, if they will be expected to share a room with someone, where they can store their belongings, and if they are allowed to "personalize" their room with color, posters, or decorations. Being offered the option to personalize their room, in some fashion, may be helpful to children who no longer have a room or space they can call their own. Having a bedroom that has been personalized to their unique interests and tastes may be one of many helpful first steps to children's adjustment and acclimation to their new home.

WHAT ARE THE HOUSE RULES?

Let's take a moment and transport ourselves again into a child's world. In Chapter 2, we reflected on the experience of having to leave our home without notice, being separated from our loved ones, and being told we were going to be placed in "foster care." We now arrive at a house where we are greeted by a strange woman standing in the doorway. She looks at us and says, "Come in. Don't be shy." We enter hesitantly as we're not quite sure what to expect. The woman walks into her kitchen and motions us forward. Without further thought, we walk forward toward the kitchen. Quickly we hear the woman say, "Dear, please remove your shoes. We don't live in a barn." We stand there embarrassed, confused, and uncomfortable. We never took our shoes off at home.

You can likely imagine how the experience can continue from here and the negative relational effects that could arise from this exchange. The caregiver may perceive the child as impolite, and the child may perceive the caregiver as mean, strange, or uninviting. The important takeaway message from this example is that household rules differ, and it's important that caregivers give children an opportunity to learn the rules before expecting children to follow them. Each household has its own culture, and it is likely that children will need to become acclimated to a new culture upon entering a new home.

HEALING SUGGESTION 3.4
C.A.R.E. FOR CHILDREN'S EXPERIENCES OF HOUSEHOLD RULES

Every household contains specific rules and/or expectations, and this structure will differ from household to household. When children enter foster care, it is likely that their new home environment will contain rules that differ from the rules in their original home environment. Children may find it helpful if the caregiver explains the rules of the home, the purpose of the rules, and how the rules may or may not differ from the rules to which they are accustomed. Some children may never have had rules in their original home. This is an important possibility that should be taken into consideration. Children who have never been exposed to household rules may not understand the purpose of rules. Explaining the importance of having household rules (e.g., they help family members stay safe, get along, and establish a structure for the home) is essential to assisting children in understanding why rules are needed.

When possible, invite children to co-create the household rules and take ownership for them. This approach affirms children's worth as competent decision-makers and provides them with opportunities to be involved in creating a safe and positive space in the household.

DO I HAVE TO DO CHORES AS SOON AS I ARRIVE?

One of the most important truths for care providers to keep in mind when caring for a child in foster care is that most children are *grieving the loss of multiple people and multiple things*. Children need people in their lives who recognize and acknowledge the losses they are experiencing and who provide them with time and support to grieve these losses.

Alicja's Experience
14 years old

Alicja's experience illustrates the impact that grief can have on children's lives and how attention and sensitivity to their losses are essential to a child's adaptation to a new home. She shares, "I first got there, and we got introduced and everything. It was almost suppertime so we ate the supper and then [the foster parents] said that we had to do dishes. My brother and sister were like really sad, and they were like, 'Well you have to do dishes,' and it was like my first hour and like the first time you go there you don't want to quickly do a chore, you want to wait a couple days and then do your chore. And they're like, 'You have to do your chore.' I was like, 'I just came here. Why don't you wait like not tomorrow but the next day and I'll do dishes. I just came here I'm not really in the mood to do dishes.' And then I like didn't do it and they were like, 'Well if you don't do dishes then you can go to your room and you can't see friends and mom and blah blah blah.' So I called my dad up and was really sad. And my dad was like, 'Just do the dishes.' And I was like, 'I don't want to do the dishes as soon as I get there.' Like no one, as soon as they get to a place, they don't want to just do dishes right then, so I was like, 'OK fine. I'll do the dishes,' and I did the dishes. And the next day I'm like, 'I can't do it today, I'm too sad to do dishes, like I can't,' and they were like, 'Well you have to do it.' I'm like, 'OK, I'll do the dishes.' "

HEALING SUGGESTION 3.5
C.A.R.E. FOR CHILDREN'S EXPERIENCES OF FOSTER
PLACEMENT ADJUSTMENT

Experiencing the sudden loss of one's family, friends, home, and belongings can completely turn an individual's world upside-down—child or adult. Children need time to adjust to their new surroundings and process the whirlwind of events and losses that have recently occurred in their lives. Care providers can exhibit sensitivity to children by supporting their need to adjust to their new home environment, acknowledging that most children are grieving multiple losses, and warmly accepting if children do not want to engage in household chores, tasks, or other activities as soon as they arrive at the home. Although some children may enjoy engaging in activities right away (all children have different styles of coping and adaptation), care providers are encouraged to support children's choices in whether they do or do not want to participate in household tasks, chores, activities, and conversations immediately upon arrival at their new home.

WHY CAN'T I SLEEP IN THE SAME ROOM AS MY SIBLING?

Children in foster care, of all ages, discuss the importance of their relationships with their siblings (Mitchell, Jones, & Renema, 2015; Mitchell & Kuczynski, 2010). Sibling relationships in foster care are an important relational connection that should not be underestimated (Unrau et al., 2008). Researchers have emphasized how children can be traumatized when they are separated from their siblings (Herrick & Piccus, 2005; Ward, 1984). Reports from children in foster care suggest that their siblings are one of the three most important relational connections in their lives (Mitchell, 2014; Mitchell et al., 2015). Many children find comfort in their relationships with their siblings and consider their sister(s) and/or brother(s) as a significant person to whom they go for emotional support (Mitchell et al., 2015). These studies illustrate how the sibling connection can be a strong and influential bond for many children, regardless of their age. During times of loss and ambiguity, it is particularly important to acknowledge the healing effect that sibling relationships can have in the lives of children in foster care.

Derrick's Experience
13 years old

Derrick recalls, "The first night they wouldn't let me and my brother sleep in the same room or whatever cause they, I don't even know. And the first night they let me sleep with him in there, and then they woke me up at 3 o'clock in the morning telling me I had to move rooms. They thought I wouldn't be able to sleep in my regular room, but then they thought I was tired enough, and then they sent me to my room. But then like a week after, they moved me to a new room and whenever I got mad at them I would just write on the back of the dressers, and they didn't even notice it."

Alicja's Experience
14 years old

Alicja also discusses how she was impacted when she was not allowed to sleep in the same room as her sibling. She shares, "It was pretty bad because they were telling me that I can't go in the room that my brother was in 'cause the girls can't go into that room 'cause it's a boy room. I was like, 'He's my brother. He's crying, and it's just him there, and he's crying. I can't take it, that's my brother, and I used to baby-sit him all the time. Let me go see him. I can't like let him cry.' And they like stuck him in the room, closed the door and locked it. I unlocked the door and was like, 'No you don't lock the door on a little kid.'"

Although not all children will desire to seek out their sibling(s) during times of distress, many children in foster care state that their siblings provide them with a source of comfort, strength, and familiarity. Derrick's and Alicja's experiences illustrate the value of recognizing and acknowledging the importance of sibling relationships during children's acclimation to their new home.

HEALING SUGGESTION 3.6
C.A.R.E. FOR SIBLING CONNECTIONS IN THE HOME

Moving into a new home can be a scary experience. When asked what it was like to live with another family, Henry (8 years old) replied, "It's scary." Children deserve to feel secure and comforted during their transition into a new home. Bedtime can elicit anxiety and fears for children experiencing traumatic stress (Yule & Williams, 1990). Because children experiencing trauma may not feel comfortable sharing their concerns and fears with adults with whom they are unfamiliar, having someone with whom they are familiar in their room, such as a sibling, may be helpful to easing children's fears and sleepless nights. Asking children if they would like to share a room with their sibling and permitting them to do so (if possible and in the best interests of the child) may ease their anxiety and fears, providing a safe haven where they can rest.

FROM THE WHERE TO THE WHO?

"Who are these people? I don't even know them."
MARK, 13 years old

Children in foster care have expressed the need for information during the time they are being relocated to their foster placement (Mitchell & Kuczynski, 2010; Unrau et al., 2008). As highlighted in this chapter, children who experience placement context ambiguity may ask questions such as "Where am I going? Will there be other children in the home? Are there pets in the home?" Once children arrive at their foster care placement, they may then begin to question the layout of the residence, where items are stored and can be located, and if their basic needs will be met. Children's reports suggest that receiving the answers to these questions prior to their arrival at their placement may be helpful in minimizing placement context ambiguity.

Upon arrival at their placement, the introduction to people and pets residing in the home, the layout of the home, and the location of necessities (e.g., food, hygiene items, garbage/recycling bins, etc.) can be helpful in acquainting children with their new home environment. Questions may arise such as "What are the house rules? When is dinnertime? Who prepares the food? Who is responsible for washing the dishes? When is my bedtime? Will someone read me a story before I go to sleep? Why can't I sleep in the same room as my sibling?" Ultimately, it is important for children to know they have adults in their lives with whom they can ask questions, openly express their concerns, and make suggestions. Moving to a new home can be a frightening experience, and children need time to process multiple factors—the loss of a home, the loss of family, the loss of friends, the loss of belongings, the acclimation to a new home environment, a new family dynamic, new expectations, and the list goes on. Creating an atmosphere that is inviting, receptive, and comfortable can assist children in adjusting to their new surroundings. As will be discussed in the next two chapters, care providers who compassionately consider and understand children's interests, opinions, needs, and experiences of loss and ambiguity during the transition into foster care can play a critical role in establishing a healthy foundation for sustainable foster care placements and valued interpersonal relationships.

Why do I have to leave?
What is foster care?
Where are you taking me?
WHO ARE THESE PEOPLE?
How about me?
When can I go home?

"I was kind of nervous about who I was going to get tooken care of and, um, who, who my foster parents are going to be."
DOMINICK, 9 years old

4

WHO Are These People?

MORE THAN 50% of children who enter the child welfare system in countries such as the United States, Canada, and England are moved to a new home to live with people who are complete strangers. Can you imagine being removed from your home and placed in a new home with people who are complete strangers? In addition to the traumatic stress experienced by many children prior to their placement in foster care, children can be further traumatized by being placed in a home with people with whom they are unfamiliar. I refer to this experience as *relationship ambiguity*—that is, a child's lack of clarity about the people with whom they have been placed (Mitchell, 2008; Mitchell & Kuczynski, 2010). In this chapter, we will explore the ways that children experience relationship ambiguity and the advice offered by children to build a relational home between care providers and the children in their care.

ARE YOU GOING TO HURT ME?

Children's reports of ambiguity suggest that relationship ambiguity is one of the most prominent experiences of ambiguity when entering foster care. Not being familiar with the adults with whom they would be living was an anxiety-provoking experience for most children. As discussed in Chapter 3, children need to feel a sense of security and safety when entering a new home. Most children are placed in foster care because they have experienced neglect and/or abuse. As a result, it is critical for children to be assured that these experiences will not reoccur with the people who are living in their new place of residence. The following reports illustrate children's experiences of relationship ambiguity.

Dominick's Experience
9 years old

Dominick explains that he was nervous about who his care providers would be. He states, "At first I was kind of like nervous about like who I was going to get tooken care of um, who, who my foster parents are going to be."

Odelia's Experience
12 years old

Odelia was afraid of "the people" when she first entered foster care. She shares, "I was scared that they weren't going to be nice to me and all that stuff." Odelia reported that she never spoke to anybody about how she was feeling. It is possible that Odelia did not feel comfortable speaking to anyone about her fears about how she would be treated in foster care or that no one invited Odelia to share with them how she was feeling.

Mark's Experience
13 years old

Mark discusses how he was uncomfortable with living with people he did not know. He states, "Whoa! My God, this is like weird and stuff. I was like, 'Who are these people? I don't even know them and I'm moving in with them' . . . I was like, 'Holy! Bring me somewhere else. I don't care where I'll have to go. I'll get locked up as long as I'm not with just some family I don't know.'" For Mark, the threat of living with a family whom he did not know was far greater than the threat of being imprisoned.

Alicja's Experience
14 years old

Alicja's experience further illustrates how children's fears of living with people they do not know could relate to their fear of further abuse and/or neglect. She states, "I was afraid they might hit me or something or they might hit my [siblings]. Like I was scared more about them. Like I don't mind if they hurt me, or whatever, but like my siblings, they're too important to get to me. So it was sort of scary for that." It is disheartening to think about how many children fear that they or their siblings will be hurt when they enter foster care and are not reassured that their new care providers will care for them, not harm them.

Sandra's Experience
10 years old

Sandra reflects on how her feelings have changed since she first entered foster care. She states, "Um, well, really, the feeling has changed 'cause I felt, like, oh, these people are probably going to abuse me. They're probably going to hit me. They probably just wanna hurt me. And like now I know that they don't wanna hurt me. They don't wanna touch me. They wanna make me safe. They wanna make me feel safe and foster care is a place where they take care of me and I can't be abused."

Social support and stable relationships are necessary in providing children with a foundation for new, trusting relationships and replacing feelings of isolation, neglect, and disconnection that they may have experienced in previous parent-child relationships. This foundation can also serve as a catalyst of support for those children who remain in the foster care system until the age of emancipation. Research has shown that being engaged in positive relationships can assist children in foster care in developing the skills and knowledge to live and function successfully on their own after exiting foster care (Courtney et al., 2001).

HEALING SUGGESTION 4.1
C.A.R.E. FOR A RELATIONAL FOUNDATION OF SECURITY,
SAFETY, AND TRUST

Care providers can assist children by notifying them immediately upon entering their new home that their home is a safe space where they will be respected, cared for, and their needs will be nurtured. In addition to understanding the meaning of foster care (i.e., it is a safe place for children to live while they are placed away from their original homes), discussed in Chapter 2, children also need to know that the adults with whom they have been placed are aware and committed to upholding this agreement.

Reports from children in foster care illustrate that children's quality of life is diminished when they do not have someone in their lives whom they can trust (Unrau et al., 2008). As one adult noted retrospectively on her placement in foster care, the inability to trust can lead to youth "subconsciously sabotaging the relationship because inside you think that it is not real, they will leave me, or they will find something wrong with me because that is the way it goes" (Unrau et al., 2008, p. 1262). Developing trusting relationships at the onset of a placement may serve as a preventive measure to allay feelings of distrust and resistance to intimacy. Unlike security and safety, which can be established immediately, trust needs to be earned. Creating a safe and secure physical environment establishes a healthy foundation upon which an emotional relationship of trust can be built.

HOW WILL YOU WELCOME ME INTO MY NEW HOME?

In the previous chapter we explored various ways that care providers can help familiarize children with their new home environment (i.e., acquainting children with the house rules, chores, etc.). Now we will focus specifically on the relational experience of *greeting* and *welcoming* children into their new home. In light of the experiences of relationship ambiguity that we just explored, it becomes apparent that an adult's initial greeting can have a significant impact on increasing or decreasing children's anxiety about the potential threat of their new home environment.

Christina's Experience
11 years old

Christina's care provider made her feel unwelcome when she first entered the home. She explains, "The [care provider] didn't seem very nice there. I don't think he said hi to me or anything there. I don't think he ever spoke to me in like three days that I was there pretty much."

Julia's Experience
15 years old

Julia also discusses how she felt uncomfortable in her new home and how she "just had to work herself in." She says, "It was weird. Like why am I at this stranger's house." When asked if she did anything to make herself feel more comfortable, she replied, "I just had to work myself in."

Alicja's Experience
14 years old

Alicja's experience also suggests that she didn't feel welcomed in the home or as part of the family. She shares, "It was like really sad, and I didn't feel like I was welcomed home, and I didn't feel like I was like a part of that family."

Craig's Experience
12 years old

Craig addresses how being in foster care and changing homes can take a toll on a child's ability to trust. He states, "At first I didn't start talking to [my care provider] right when I went there because I couldn't really trust her yet. I needed to know I could trust her. That's the thing. If you have been in so many different homes, you don't know who you can trust and who you can love and stuff like that." Craig's experience speaks to the reality that feeling uncomfortable in a new home is not limited to a child's first foster care placement. With every new placement, it can get increasingly harder for a child to trust and know "who you can love."

Odelia's Advice
12 years old

Odelia provides advice to care providers who are preparing to welcome a child to their home. She states, "[The child] is probably like really nervous about meeting you, too, and maybe they are excited, but I'm sure they don't like being taken away from their family so they're probably like really scared so I'd be as nice as you can to them." Odelia addresses the fears that children can have when they enter a new home and encourages care providers to be considerate of a child's feelings and be "as nice as you can to them."

Toni's Advice
18 years old

Toni believes it's important for care providers to be sensitive to children's attitudes when they first enter the home as the presenting attitude may not be indicative of the child's personality or regular behavior. She states, "My advice is not to judge a book by its cover. Just because a youth may come in with an attitude or really upset, you should not judge them or be like, 'What's wrong with you?' or feel like they have naturally an attitude. You have to realize that they just went through a traumatizing event."

Tywan's Advice
18 years old

Tywan expresses the importance for care providers to take the time to communicate with children once they are placed in their care. He advises, "[Care providers] should just take some time out of their day. Not the first day exactly, 'cause the first time is really, it's a time of trial. Just take some time out the third or fourth day to actually sit down and talk to the [child in their care] and let them know that, you know, what has happened has already happened and that that's not gonna affect them here, that's not gonna determine where they land from here on out. And it's just, it's a clean slate, so let's start fresh."

HEALING SUGGESTION 4.2
C.A.R.E. FOR A WELCOMING HOME ATMOSPHERE

Children's reports suggest that the initial greeting they receive from their new caregivers can have a lasting impact on them. Many children are consumed with fear, trepidation, and anxiety as they enter into their new home environment. Providing a welcoming atmosphere may minimize feelings of concern, imposition, and fears of repeated abuse or neglect. Although it is hoped that children will be notified of the meaning and purpose of the foster care system (Healing Suggestion 2.1 in Chapter 2) upon being told of the need to be placed in foster care, this information can be further solidified and supported by children receiving a warm and welcoming greeting from their new caregivers. Because children may be upset, fearful, anxious, and grieving, the most appropriate greeting will be child-specific. Regardless of the situation, however, welcoming children with kindness and a smile, advising them that you are there for them if they have any questions or need anything, reminding them that the home is a safe space where their needs will be met, and acknowledging that their presence in the home is welcome and not an inconvenience can be helpful ways to greet and welcome children into their new home.

WILL YOU CARE FOR ME THE SAME WAY YOU CARE FOR YOUR BIOLOGICAL CHILDREN?

Children's reports in my studies as well as other studies (Butler & Charles, 1999) suggest that some care providers in foster homes exhibit preferential treatment of their biological children. This is disconcerting, as children can readily detect inequality. We likely can hear familiar cries from our own childhood experiences, "Why does he get to go with you and I can't?" "I want some ice cream too!" and "That's my toy!"

The reports that follow illustrate children's experiences of caregivers' preferential treatment of children.

Nicholas's Experience
13 years old

Nicholas reports, "[My care provider] kind of spoils the other guys. She hasn't bought me any piece of clothing yet. [It makes me feel] not liked. My mom has to buy me all the clothing, and I think it's funny because [my care provider] is not that money-wise because the agency pays for it. It's just that I don't know. She buys the boys things. Everything else but like, my shoes, like, um, they're like badly old. I asked her to buy me a pair of shoes and she says, 'Get your mom to buy you shoes because she likes buying you stuff.' She doesn't. It's just 'cause she has to because [my care provider] doesn't buy my anything, so finally my [case]worker bought me shoes.'"

Mark's Experience
13 years old

Mark recalls his first placement, "The first place, like, I wanted out of there. They should look out for the people they pick because these people were like, 'You can clean up the chicken poop, clean up all this, do this, do that' and it looked like they just wanted me and this other boy there so we could work and their real son was riding horses, doing all this stuff, and we're just like, got told to make a bit of money and then we can like maybe save it for a pony or something. And I'm like, 'I'm not into that.' Got to clean up the chicken poop and stuff. I went into the bedroom to go to sleep and the blankets and everything in there smelt like disgusting. It was like weird in there, so I was like freaking out. And [the child welfare agency] was like, 'These are one of the top people you are going with. They're really good people.' And I'm like, 'Alright.' It was pretty weird."

Alicja's Experience
14 years old

Alicja shares, "The difference was that [my current care provider] treated us like we're hers, like we're her kids. She didn't treat us like not equally with her kids, she treated us the same. But like the other two [foster placements] treated us like 'Whatever, you're not my kids. I just feed you and you sleep and everything and you're fine.' Like [my current care provider], she made sure we had what we need and all that stuff and it was pretty cool."

Quez's Experience
20 years old

Quez discusses how his care providers treated him "like any other family member." He states, "My experience is my foster parents were always good to me.

So I really didn't have any problems. They made sure I had everything. They really helped me out. They made sure I was into sports, had all my funds for sports and school and just made me like I was part of the family and didn't even say, 'He's a foster child.' They said, 'This is my son,' and they just treated me like another family member." As Quez notes, being referred to as "a son" rather than "a foster child" can make a meaningful difference in a child's life.

Josh's Advice
21 years old

Josh addresses the need for children to be treated equally and valued and accepted for who they are. He states, "I think as far as being a youth in foster care, a youth wants to be accepted. Like you have to treat every youth equally no matter if they are in foster care or not, because at the end of the day they all want to be accepted." Ultimately, all children deserve to be valued and loved.

HEALING SUGGESTION 4.3
C.A.R.E. FOR EQUAL TREATMENT OF CHILDREN IN THE HOME

Navigating the fair and equal treatment of children within a household is not isolated to foster care settings; however, this assurance is particularly important for children in foster care. Children who are not the caregivers' biological or adopted children may quickly interpret unequal treatment as reflective of their being less important, less valued, and, sadly, less loved. In a home that is expected to be a child's safe haven from neglect and abuse, it is particularly important for children to feel they are important, valued, and loved.

Care providers are encouraged to be mindful of how children who have been subjected to and traumatized by abuse and neglect can be particularly re-traumatized by further acts of exclusion or maltreatment. Promoting a home environment of equal treatment, unconditional love, and respect for all family members is essential for a healthy family dynamic. All children deserve to feel appreciated, acknowledged, respected, and treated equally to the other children in the home.

WILL YOU COMMUNICATE WITH ME RESPECTFULLY?

Respectful intercommunication between children and their care providers is a recurring theme that emerges from reports by children in foster care. Children discuss how certain forms of intercommunication can be more effective than others. For example, as the following reports illustrate, name-calling and yelling can negatively impact a relationship, whereas respectful and reflective dialogue can promote positive outcomes.

Alicja's Experience
14 years old

Alicja's experience illustrates how respectful communication is far more effective than disrespectful communication with children. She states, "[My care providers] treated me like I was some weird person who came into the house or something. They like called me fat and mean words like that and I was like 'I'm not fat' and then I started thinking it. And my dad's like, 'You're not fat! Stop saying that,' and I was like, 'Oh yeah I am, cause [my care provider] is saying that,' and my dad was like, 'What?' and my dad got upset because she was calling me fat and that's not right to say that. And she was telling me I had to lose weight and stuff and I was like, 'Isn't that for a doctor to say?' and then my brother started saying it with her and like I don't like calling people fat but when she was calling me fat, she was sort of fat. So I was like, 'Well look at yourself like, don't say it to me, look at yourself.' But I'm not like that so I was like, 'Oh alright.' And then my brother started calling me it and I was like 'Ah! This is not OK.' Alicja asked to live with another care provider and was moved to a new home. She is now "happy because [her care provider] is like really nice. She might get like mad or something but all parents get mad so it's pretty easy and stuff. If we're sad or something she'll talk to us about it and like when we're at home and stuff she'll talk to us and watch movies with us and buy us stuff and go shopping and everything so it's pretty cool."

Donnie's Experience
12 years old

Donnie explains how his care provider is "sometimes really grumpy. Sometimes she goes like RAH, you know like, we accidentally drop something or like knock over a lamp. Cause like there's this chair upstairs that always like hits the table and the table only has three legs. It's designed for it and she's like RAH, and we always say 'OK, like leave it be and try not to knock it.'" Donnie shares that it makes him feel "kinda crappy" when she communicates to him in this way and that he would prefer that his care provider say, "Please don't knock that."

Denise's Experience
13 years old

Although Denise's care provider is "really nice" she sometimes feels like she can't talk to her "when she gets mad. [My care provider] kind of freaks me out, just a little bit. I ask her not to be rude to me, because if she is being rude to me I automatically will be rude back and that will get her more angry and I don't want that happening 'cause once I take my temper out, I can over, I could over out-yell her so that would be just not cool." Denise explains that children, as well as their care providers, need to be mindful of how they communicate with one another. Being rude or out-yelling one another is "just not cool."

Craig's Advice
12 years old

Craig reports that disrespectful communication can be hurtful to children. He shares, "It hurts a lot when we yell at each other." Craig prefers "not yelling" and believes that it would be better to "take deep breaths or tell each other to calm down and stuff like that or walk away and stay away from each other for a bit."

Odelia's Advice
12 years old

Odelia also believes it is valuable to invest in productive, positive communication. She advises care providers to "be as nice as you can to them and just if you ask them to do something and they don't do it, then, confront them nicely. Don't just like, I'm sure that you might be angry and you might want to yell at them but try not to as hard as you can 'cause that'll make them feel a lot worse about you, and I'm sure that you want them to like you."

Cheyenne's Advice
18 years old

Cheyenne identifies respect as a necessary ingredient for effective communication. She explains, "Respect goes a very long way with me. That was one of the problems that me and my caregivers had. I feel like if I give you respect then I deserve to have it, too. It goes both ways. When I moved into the group home, me and one of the girls there, we got real close. One day she just couldn't take it so she just walked out the door. I was trying to stop her because I knew if anybody in the house could stop her, it would have been me. One of the [staff] there was like, 'Stop, if you go out that door you're gonna get a reminder.' That's the point system. It really got on my nerves a lot. And then a few hours later, [my friend] came back, and she just came straight to me and started hugging me. That same [staff] said, 'Cheyenne, you need to go to your room because this is not your business.' I looked at her and I said, 'I'm gonna stay here and comfort my friend because that's what friends are for. You're not gonna give me a reminder either because you're teaching me not to show emotion towards people and not to care for people, and when the going gets rough, you turn away, you turn your back on them.' I don't think that was helpful for anybody because if you're [a caregiver], you need to be teaching people compassion. If you have a job caring for children, show that you care and not the opposite.

If you want to have this job you need to actually care about children. I called my caseworker because [the staff] was trying to give me a reminder for that, and I would have gotten in a lot of trouble for not going to my room. My case manager called the group home that I was staying at, and she advocated on my side because I didn't end up getting in trouble because she thought that I was in the right. I think that was probably the most helpful thing that she could have done because I don't think anybody would have heard what I really had to say had I not called my caseworker."

Michelle's Advice
21 years old

Michelle reflects on the importance of patience, understanding, and compassion in communication. She states, "I feel like [in foster care], I went through not really so much physical abuse; it was more so mentally and emotionally. I honestly felt like I was being abused while I was in care too because if I did not know an answer, I would get like, sarcasm. Like, 'OK, well why don't you know this?' If I was never taught it, then I'm not going to know it. And so I felt like while I was in care, there were some sarcastic moments where I felt like people were just nitpicking and picking at me and then like the only way I could, the only way I knew how to like get away from it was going in my room and like sheltering myself or running away. And when I ran away, I caused a scene and when I did something that was like out of pocket [out of the ordinary], they looked at me differently, because I didn't know what I was getting in trouble for. I didn't know. My thing was, growing up, if I didn't know the answer, [I was] to ask. Sometimes I do ask things with intentions to be funny and just to get on someone's nerves, but when I honestly did not know the question, and then I felt like [I would hear], 'Oh you're grown. You should know this.' Yes, I'm grown because I've been doing everything all myself, but like, even grown people ask questions. And I felt like that was, like a misunderstanding, while I was in care. And so I felt like I went through some type of abuse while I was in care. [Care providers] should look at things from different points of views, and then instead of just jumping down someone's throat, they have to be open and just have to be like, 'OK, well, maybe they don't know that.' They just have to be open to like different backgrounds." Michelle conveys how children may feel misunderstood or embarrassed when they ask questions about "things they should already know." She advises care providers to consider that children may not know the answers to the questions they are asking, as simple as the answers may seem. Affirming a child's worth involves being patient, listening to and answering the questions that have been raised, not making a child feel incompetent or embarrassed for asking questions, and acknowledging that answers that appear to be "obvious" may not be so obvious to the child asking the question.

HEALING SUGGESTION 4.4
C.A.R.E. FOR RESPECTFUL COMMUNICATION

Care providers are asked to remain mindful of effective communication styles. The importance of speaking respectfully with children was echoed in many of the children's reports. Children often mirror the behavior of the adults in their lives. Care providers are encouraged to model the type of behavior and communication style that they would like to elicit from the children in their household. Implementing an approach that involves patience, respect, humility, and compassion can be helpful to effective parent-child intercommunication and conflict management.

WILL YOU GIVE UP ON ME?

In addition to attending to the needs of children during the first days and weeks of their transition into foster care and new residences, children also need to know that the adults in their lives will be constantly invested in their well-being. Some children may be hesitant to open up or trust their new caregivers right away, and time is

---

HEALING SUGGESTION 4.5
C.A.R.E. FOR CONSTANT LOVE AND SUPPORT

As children enter foster care and are introduced to new relationships and family structures, the provision of time and understanding can be helpful during their transition. It may be particularly helpful for care providers to keep checking in with children to see how they are doing and if they have any questions or concerns. Because separation from loved ones can bring with it highs and lows on any given day, it is important for children to know that they always have someone to whom they can go when they are in need. It is also essential that children know that their care providers are invested in their caring relationship and will not give up on them. Building on the suggestions provided in this and previous chapters, care providers can encourage children by keeping the lines of communication open and having frequent conversations with children about their needs, their concerns, their interests, and their feelings. Children, especially children in foster care, need to know that they are not a burden, that they are accepted, that they belong, and that they are loved. Attending to children's needs at the beginning and throughout their placement can create a space for children to thrive, grow, and heal.

---

needed for them to adapt to their new home environment. Providing children with constant support, encouragement, love, and understanding are essential building blocks for building a relational home.

FROM THE WHO TO THE HOW?

In this chapter, we explored the dynamics of new caregiver-child relationships and ways to promote a household atmosphere and family dynamic based on security, safety, and trust. Children who have experienced abuse and neglect are yearning for a home environment that will be welcoming, encouraging, and loving. Care providers can create this space by communicating with children about their interests, encouraging equality in the household, refraining from parental favoritism, and engaging in respectful communication.

As children adapt to their new family surroundings and feel assured that their basic needs will be met (e.g., they will be fed, they will be clothed, they will have a roof over their head, they will be protected by their care providers), a deeper and more intrinsic question surfaces in their minds. In our journey, thus far, we have explored children's questions about their physical and relational environments. In the next chapter, we will venture into children's inner environments, exploring their questions about the nurturance, acceptance, and continuity of self.

Why do I have to leave?
What is foster care?
Where are you taking me?
Who are these people?
HOW ABOUT ME?
When can I go home?

"I didn't care. I thought I was screwed over for the rest of my life."
MARK, 13 years old

5

How About ME?

HOW DO CHILDREN make sense of their inner and interpersonal worlds when events turn their lives upside down? In the previous chapters we examined how children in foster care search for answers to understand the meaning of foster care, the purpose of their placement in foster care, their home environment, and the people with whom they will be living. We have focused on their search to understand the meaning, people, and surroundings in their new world. As children enter the foster care system and hear themselves referred to as a "foster child" instead of "child," they may begin to question what this new label means in respect to who they are, who they were, and who they are going to be. In this chapter, we explore how being placed in foster care creates a shift in a child's inner and interpersonal world and how care providers can tend to a child's inner world during this significant life transition.

AM I STILL A DAUGHTER/SON, A SISTER/BROTHER, A FRIEND?

Our roles in life contribute greatly to our understanding of who we are and how we engage with the world. Let's take a moment to think about this. Draw your attention to a role in your life that you currently have (e.g., a parent, a child, or an older/younger sibling) and take a moment to consider how this relationship contributes to your identity. Now imagine what your life would be like if the person who creates an opportunity for you to serve in that role no longer existed. How would this change impact your identity and your reality? Consider, then, how a child's world drastically changes within only moments of being placed in foster care.

Robert's Experience
20 years old

Robert recalls the day he was removed from his family, the questions he wanted answered, and how his world was turned upside-down. He shares, "When [the Department of Social Services] came into my home and took us away from our family, I was thinking, 'Was I still gonna have my brothers and my sister?' I went into care not knowing where I would go or who I would be staying with and that was tough for me because I didn't know where my parents would be. Mentally I thought like, they were far away, but physically they were right around the corner from me. And that kinda drove me insane for a while. I did have my brother with me, so that kinda comforted me a little bit, having him with me, but we eventually got separated. And my sister, they took her away from me when we first got to care, so I didn't have no sister. And my friends, I didn't have any friends either. All I had was my brother. He was my only friend in care. So, how about me?"

It is not uncommon for children to question their role within a new family or social context once they have been separated from their families. For example, children who are the oldest sibling in their original family may begin to question their role as a sibling when they are placed in a new family environment where all of the other children are older. These children may be used to playing the role of a "big brother" or "big sister" and believe their identity is being challenged and/or threatened within a new family environment where there are no younger siblings present and it is no longer possible for them to fulfill this role.

Children who experience role ambiguity (i.e., a lack of clarity about one's role in an interpersonal context) can experience negative effects from displacement and being considered the "other." For example, Kools (1997) interviewed 17 adolescents in foster care, 15 to 19 years of age, and discussed how being a "foster child" can carry with it a diminished societal and [familial] status, negative stigma, and depersonalization. The following quote authentically depicts a child's experience of role ambiguity:

> I want to go over there and visit some of my family and relatives. I don't want to forget about my culture and stuff so I want to go there. But it's not easy when you are in foster care. It's like you're not part of that anymore; like they're not your family anymore. I mean, they're still your family but not like they used to be. You know? And, it's easy to forget where you came from, who you are. (Kools, 1997, p. 268)

Other researchers have highlighted how children can experience loyalty conflicts when trying to consolidate their role as a "child" with their foster parents as well as with their original parents (Leathers, 2003). Research has also shown that some children may experience role strain within the family unit when they do not conceptualize their foster family to be a part of their interpersonal future (Butler & Charles, 1999). The experience of feeling disconnected and displaced within a family unit can be stressful for children who are in need of love and supportive, nurturing adults in their lives. Ultimately, when trying to navigate their way in a new family environment, children can be faced with many challenges to their identity while trying to determine how to effectively engage in their perceived roles and interact in their interpersonal world.

HEALING SUGGESTION 5.1
C.A.R.E FOR CHILDREN'S EXPERIENCES OF ROLE AMBIGUITY

Children's identities are constantly threatened and challenged as they enter and navigate the foster care system. Care providers can assist children by asking them about their perceived roles in life and the importance of these roles. If a child has been separated from a sibling and strongly identifies with the role of being a sister/brother, care providers can consider how to help a child maintain his or her identity even though the sibling may no longer reside in the home. There are many roles with which a child may identify: being a child, a sibling, a grandchild, a friend, a neighbor, a niece/ nephew, a student, an athlete, a musician, and so forth. Care providers can contribute to a child's healing by simply recognizing, acknowledging, and supporting the roles in a child's life that are perceived as significant. Providing children with opportunities to nurture perceived roles that are healthy can be helpful to children who are struggling to find stability and consistency in their lives. In addition to attending to a child's experience of role ambiguity, it is also important for care providers to attend to the losses that have contributed to this experience of ambiguity. In the next chapter, we will discuss how to assist children who are coping with relationship losses (including ambiguous loss) and boundary ambiguity (Boss, 1999) within their original families.

HOW WILL YOU INVEST IN ME AND MY INTERESTS?

Creating an interpersonal environment that acknowledges the interests of children and assures them that their new care providers are genuinely interested in getting to know them is essential to building a relational home. Because trust has not yet been established, offering children an opportunity to build this relationship with their care providers can be a critical first step to building a healthy and respectful caregiver-child relationship. The following reports highlight the importance of investing in building a relational home with children when they are first placed in foster care.

Christina's Advice
11 years old

Christina suggests that care providers communicate with children and spend some time getting to know them. She states, "Ask, 'Do you want to talk or anything?' And, like they don't necessarily have to 'cause of an issue they wouldn't really want to talk about at all . . . Maybe you wanna ask them if they wanna go out, maybe, um, you can go and get some stuff. Clothes, get a few things, it doesn't have to necessarily need to be clothes. Maybe you could go out and get, like go out and get an ice cream or . . . And just like introduce yourself to each other and tell each other a little bit about each other and stuff."

Miguel's Advice
8 years old

Miguel offers advice to care providers about ways they can help children to feel welcome in their new home. He suggests, "Get a stuffed animal for them. Be nice to them. Let them have junk food. Let them play outside and meet new friends. Get a dog for them. Um, go to the park with them. Let them have ice cream."

Brenda's Advice
11 years old

Brenda also discusses the value of care providers spending time with children and investing in getting to know them. She states, "Get to know them a bit like sitting on the couch, um, watching TV. During commercials you can ask them questions like what's their favorite animal, what's their favorite color, what's their favorite food. Get to know them a little bit better, so they can know what they like. Cause like when I first came to foster care, um, I was a bit shy, but she didn't ask me anything and I ate something that like, made me throw up after. I was like 'I hate this stuff.'" As Brenda shares, a simple conversation about what she could, and could not, eat would have been helpful to building a relationship of care with her new care providers.

Alicja's Advice
14 years old

Alicja highlights the importance of learning about the child's needs and interests. She advises, "I would tell you to ask her what she likes and what she doesn't like or he or she or whatever. And take them out somewhere to McDonalds or something and then take them out swimming or to the park or something that would be fun—shopping or something that they like to do. And talk to them and ask them what they would like to do for a week or what they would like to do today or something and try to show them their room and show them their house. Tell them that they could get food, that they can eat anything. Eat whatever they want to eat."

Donnie's Advice
12 years old

Donnie advises care providers to "suck up" to children. He says, "Try to suck up by giving them presents. Welcome presents. Or you could, treat her like you're cool. First you bring her out for dinner to like, what's that restaurant (pause) I forget the restaurant, just say McDonalds. Then say what's your favorite color and ask her questions about her life and tell her what you think about, so the [care provider] tells the kid about her life and how it's alike. And tell her how she felt when she was a little kid too." Donnie's advice also illustrates how a relational home can be built when care providers share their own interests and experiences as well as asking children about themselves. By sharing their thoughts and experiences with children, care providers demonstrate to children that they are willing to be open and vulnerable, too.

Khadeja's Advice
20 years old

Khadeja's advice addresses experiences when care providers pay more attention to what they read in a child's case report or hear from other adults than what they learn directly from the child. She advises, "Each child is different. When it comes into relations with foster care, you shouldn't always go upon what you hear because not everyone knows the true story. You should pretty much get to know the youth before you decide to throw in their face what you think you know because of what you heard [or read] somewhere." Khadeja emphasizes the importance of communicating with children directly and not drawing assumptions about them based on reports from others.

Angela's Experience
12 years old

Angela's experience validates the importance of investing in children and building a relational home. She reflects, "Before, I felt that I couldn't talk to [my care provider]. Stuff like that. But, now me and [my care provider] have like heart-to-heart conversations like all the time."

Children express the need for care providers to establish a rapport with children who are placed in their safekeeping. Asking children questions about their interests can be a good first step in establishing a relationship built on openness, acceptance, and mutual respect. When children are asked about their interests, they are also hearing phrases such as, "I value you," "I care about what is important to you," "I am interested in learning about things that make you happy," and "I do not want to impose my beliefs on you about what is important to you or what makes you happy." The underlying healing messages implicit in asking children about their interests are abundant in nurturance, acceptance, love, and care.

Once care providers have learned what is significant to children, they can then move forward and take the necessary steps to invest in these interests. It is important to note that *investing* is not limited to providing financial support for children to pursue activities and commitments. Children need and deserve emotional and physical investment, too. Attending children's tournaments and cheering them on from the sidelines, driving children to their music lessons and sitting patiently as they learn their musical scales, drying children's tears after they lose a competition that meant a lot to them and reminding them that everyone wins on some level are just a few examples that illustrate how caregivers can be present and invested in a child's life. By identifying and investing in the interests and commitments of a child, caregivers can become a source of encouragement and a catalyst of inspiration.

HEALING SUGGESTION 5.2
C.A.R.E. FOR CHILDREN'S INTERESTS AND COMMITMENTS

Care providers are encouraged to communicate with children about their interests, their commitments, their hobbies, and other matters of importance as they navigate their way into and through the child welfare system. Because the transition into foster care can disrupt many facets of a child's inner and interpersonal worlds, it can be helpful for children to have opportunities to maintain commitments and interests that need not be disrupted. Care providers can communicate with children about their likes and dislikes and other relevant information to learn what is important to them. A useful tool to engage in this conversation is the "About Me" form, developed by FosterClub, a national network for young people in foster care (www.fosterclub.com/sites/default/files/About_Me.pdf). This conversation can also generate discussion about the likes and dislikes of care providers. Youth in foster care have reported that they actively seek emotional support and advice from adults in their lives who have had similar experiences (Mitchell, 2014). Ultimately, learning about shared interests and commonalities can build a relational home based on mutual understanding and trust. This activity may also reduce children's stressful appraisals by demonstrating to them that their needs, values, and commitments will be acknowledged, considered, and nurtured by their new caregivers.

During the first few days of a child's transition to their new home, care providers are encouraged to cook a child's favorite meal, ask children if they would like help setting up their room, arrange a home "premiere" of the child's favorite age-friendly television program or movie, and/or other activities deemed important by children that can help to demonstrate to them that their interests are respected and welcomed in the new household.

HOW DO I MAINTAIN OR ESTABLISH FRIENDSHIPS?

Children who are placed in foster care are often faced with the need to form new friendships due to their relocation to a new home. Peer relationships are a critical component of a child's development (Parker, Rubin, Erarth, Wojslawowicz, & Buskirk, 2006), and the absence of friendships in a child's life can result in feelings of loneliness, depression, low self-esteem, and rejection (Parker et al., 2006). As illustrated in the following reports, friendships play a meaningful role in a child's world.

Henry's Experience
8 years old

During his interview, Henry explains that he had to start a new school and his friends did not go to the new school with him. Henry recalls how difficult it was to make friends at first but now he has plenty. He shares, "It took me all summer to get friends, but now I have so many."

Alicja's Experience
14 years old

When asked what the best thing was for her since she moved into foster care, Alicja replies, "Meeting new friends." Alicja identifies that having the opportunity to make new friends is one of the benefits of foster care.

Miguel's Experience
8 years old

Similar to Alicja, Miguel identifies friendship as helpful supports to a child's adaptation to foster care. When asked what was helpful to him when entering foster care, Miguel replies, "I like foster care because I like playing with my friends."

Odelia's Experience
12 years old

Odelia addresses the importance of not only having friends but also the ability to maintain friendships while in foster care. She reports, "I don't have a very close relationship with [my caregivers], so, it's not like I want to do anything with them. And so, you know how I'm used to having siblings and stuff so I'll want to hang out with my friends and stuff because I'm the only kid there and it's really boring. Just to be doing things by yourself all day. So I always like to have my friends over and [my caregiver] gets mad when I want sleepovers. I don't know why. She calls it the White Motel and I tell her, 'Well, why do you think it's that? It's just a sleepover. Lots of girls want sleepovers when they're like kids. I don't know, maybe when she was little she didn't get that, but, things change . . . She just hates it when I want to have a sleepover and she simply says 'No, absolutely not.' She gets really mad." Some children, like Odelia, may find it particularly difficult when they are separated from their siblings in foster care and are placed in a home without other children. The value of friendships, and the role they can serve in children's lives, especially for those children who have been separated from their siblings, should not be underestimated. Communicating, affirming, and recognizing the role friendships play in children's lives and attending to children's needs are essential to building a relational home.

Christina's Experience
11 years old

Christina discusses how some foster care placements can present challenges to children maintaining their friendships because of where the home is located. She reports, "It's a pain in the butt, 'cause I'm like in the middle of nowhere, from my friends."

Nicholas's Experience
13 years old

Similar to Christina, Nicholas also reports the difficulties he experiences because of the location of his placement. When he moved to his new home he did not keep in touch with his friends because "they're too far." When he asked if someone could drive him to visit his friends, "they said it's too far to drive." Nicholas advises for children entering foster care to "make as many friends as possible."

Mark's Advice
13 years old

Mark's advice echoes the advice offered by Nicholas, "find a kid or something. Hang out with some kids."

Gabriella's Advice
12 years old

A helpful strategy for care providers interested in welcoming children to their new home is to honor children's friendships. When asked what would help children feel welcome, Gabriella replies, "Maybe to have my friends come over or I could go to their house and stuff." By providing children with opportunities to spend time with their friends, care providers communicate to children that they care about the relationships that are significant to the child and are willing to ensure that their relational needs are nurtured.

HEALING SUGGESTION 5.3
C.A.R.E. FOR CHILDREN'S FRIENDSHIPS

Acknowledging the importance of friendships in a child's life can present an enriching opportunity to connect and build relationships with other children. Children value the unique role that friendships serve in their lives, and receiving support from care providers in regard to their friendships can demonstrate to children that this component of their world will be nurtured during their transition into a new home environment. Care providers can encourage children to develop new friendships as well as maintain their existing friendships through various methods, such as providing children with the means to send mail/email (e.g., paper, envelopes, stamps, or email account), involving children in leisure activities and social groups, and, as many children expressed, permitting sleepovers can be a favorite among children! Whatever the means, it is essential that children are able to sense and witness that efforts will be made by the adults in their lives to assist them in maintaining and forming new peer relationships. Unfortunately, sometimes it is not possible for children to maintain all of their friendships once they are relocated to a new home. In Chapter 6, we explore in greater detail how to care for children as they grieve the loss of relationships.

HOW WILL MY FEELINGS AND OPINIONS BE INCLUDED
IN THE DECISIONS THAT AFFECT ME?

There are numerous decisions that are made by adults that affect children's lives. When children are placed in foster care, care providers make decisions about where children will attend school, with whom and how often children will have scheduled visits, where children will live, and the list goes on. Children's reports illustrate how being included in decision-making opportunities helps to build a relational home between them and their care providers.

Tracey's Experience
23 years old

Tracey discusses the benefits of children being invited to decorate or personalize their room. She shares, "When I first came into foster care, the first foster home I went into, I was stuck in a room with three other girls. [My foster parents] didn't ask me if I wanted to be in another room, um, not that they had any other rooms. I had to be on a bunk bed, and I had to be on the bottom because I was the oldest. They didn't ask my opinion on whether I wanted to do anything differently or whether they had any other options. Another home that I went into had a bed in the middle. In the morning when I got up, I had to put everything in the closet. She wouldn't let me change the room around. It was not helpful to me not getting my opinion on how I wanted my room to be, because I didn't have a lot of the things that I came into foster care with. One home that I went to I specifically addressed the fact that I wanted to have my own room before I moved in. This foster family picked out the color that I liked and painted the room before I moved in and then let me decorate the room however I wanted to. That was really helpful." As Tracey shared, she "didn't have a lot of the things that she came into foster care with." Being invited to contribute their own personal touch to their room can have a lot more meaning to children than just picking colors; it can validate to children that they and their opinions are valued by their care providers.

Dominick's Advice
9 years old

Dominick believes that communicating with children about their needs and wants is helpful for children entering foster care. He advises, "Ask them any questions, like if you want. Like say, like how my lawyer does. She lets you say anything that you want to for foster care, like, have a visit or something like that."

Angela's Advice
12 years old

Angela suggests that care providers allow children to select the school they will attend. She states, "I think that [children] should have an opportunity to visit a whole bunch of different schools and then choose which one they want to go to."

Derrick's Advice
13 years old

Similar to other children's reports, Derrick believes that communicating with children and offering them choices can help them feel comfortable in their new home. He advises, "Let them choose what they want for supper . . . Ask them what color they'd like their room or something and then paint it that color." Derrick's advice echoes Tracey's experience; providing children with choices and opportunities to express their interests and personal preferences can nurture children's inner worlds.

HEALING SUGGESTION 5.4
C.A.R.E. FOR INVITING, INVOLVING, AND ENGAGING CHILDREN
IN DECISION-MAKING OPPORTUNITIES

The value of including children in the decisions that affect their lives is evident in research (van Bijleveld, Dedding, & Bunders-Aelen, 2015). Providing an opportunity for children to decide on matters of importance to them can help to build self-esteem, competence, and trust (Vis, Strandbu, Holtan, & Thomas, 2011). Children can encourage care providers to include them in any decisions that will directly impact their inner and interpersonal worlds. For example, children can provide valuable input on decisions involving what school they will attend, what color they would like their room to be, what social activities they would like to be involved in, and which relatives and friends they would like to spend time with. Actively listening to children's viewpoints and preferences in relation to matters that directly affect them can enhance the caregiver-child relationship by demonstrating to children that their opinions are important and valued, their feelings are being recognized and acknowledged, and they are considered by care providers as competent contributors to the decision-making process.

HOW WILL YOU CARE FOR MY SPIRITUALITY
AND SPIRITUAL NEEDS?

Spirituality, which can include one's religious and existential beliefs, can be an important part of the lives of children in foster care (Jackson et al., 2010; Mitchell,

Silver, & Ross, 2012; Whiting & Lee, 2003). Findings from my most recent study indicate that 86% of youth transitioning out of foster care (n=223) identified their spiritual beliefs as important or very important to them (Mitchell, Vann, & Jones, 2014). Preliminary reports from this research suggest that spirituality can be an important healing resource that contributes to the emotional well-being of children in foster care. As one youth reported, "[My spirituality] brought me out of trouble, turned my life around, and taught me a lot of wisdom." Spirituality is an integral component of children's lives, especially children in foster care (DiLorenzo & Nix-Early, 2004). Furthermore, because spirituality is an important dimension of child well-being (Urry & Poey, 2008), it is important for adults to care for and nurture this part of a child's identity.

HEALING SUGGESTION 5.5
C.A.R.E. FOR CHILDREN'S SPIRITUAL BELIEFS

Spirituality can be a personal and sensitive subject matter. Everyone has his or her own experiences and beliefs. This truth does not discriminate based on gender, ethnicity, or age. Like many adults, children are also exploring their understanding of existence, the world around them, and their role in the world. Some children will connect with a particular religion or religions, whereas others may choose not to explore their spirituality through an organized religion. Spirituality can be explored through music, nature, art, animals, connections with others, and the list goes on! Care providers can demonstrate their care for children's spiritual beliefs by communicating with children about their spiritual beliefs, thoughts, and interests and allowing children to practice and explore their spirituality in a supportive and nurturing environment. Sometimes children's belief systems will differ from the beliefs of their care providers. It is essential to note that children have the right to examine and practice their own personal spiritual beliefs (United Nations Convention on the Rights of the Child, Article 14, 1989), and care providers should support children's spiritual explorations. Caring for children's spiritual beliefs can include engaging in respectful dialogue with children about their spiritual beliefs, encouraging children to participate in activities that nurture their spiritual interests, providing transportation to spiritual events, and being open to new spiritual insights, ideas, and inquiries that emerge for children as they grow and mature.

WHOM CAN I TALK WITH ABOUT HOW I AM FEELING?

Jessica's Experience
12 years old

Some children, like Jessica, do not openly communicate when they are distressed. She states, "I don't tell anything. I just keep it in my head." It was not clear from the report whether Jessica kept her feelings to herself because of her own personal choice or because she was not offered opportunities from others to share her feelings with them.

Odelia's Experience
12 years old

Odelia discusses how she feels when her foster parents don't communicate and listen to her feelings. She explains, "Yeah, my mom made a mistake, but I think she's trying hard, but nobody really wants to listen to me say that. They don't really care. They'll just say 'Oh yeah, but you gotta understand, your mom's not doing good.' Yeah, I know, but she's still trying her best. Like you guys don't get that, you just think, 'Oh, she's not doing this right,' so look they don't care. Right. So, I don't get why they do that kind of thing . . . It kinda really makes me sad, like, like I wanna cry, but I don't cry. It just sits in me, and it just makes me think, and I'm sad."

Henry's Experience
8 years old

When asked if he ever tells anyone about how he feels about things, Henry replies, "No." He sometimes tells his care provider how he feels but never speaks to his siblings about his feelings. They also don't talk to him about how they are feeling. When asked if he ever speaks to his mother about his feelings, he replies, "No." Henry advises that his mom never asks him about his feelings but, if she did ask him, he would express his feelings to her.

Jazmine's Advice
18 years old

Having a counselor can be an essential resource for children who are coping with trauma and challenging situations. Jazmine reflects, "The only way I think I had been able to deal and cope with things in my life is counseling. [My counselor] taught me how to express my feelings instead of just holding everything in, because I used to just be like, I would not tell nobody nothing. I hold so much stuff in. It's like any little thing that just ticked me off, like annoyed me, I'd just like go off. [My counselor] taught me how to cope. So you know, I think that's how foster parents or caseworkers should do for more children, but I mean counseling, I mean it's not something 'cause they are crazy or psychotic or something like that, I think it would help kids just to have somebody listen to them. And that's all that kids in foster care want because that's what I wanted."

HEALING SUGGESTION 5.6
C.A.R.E. FOR CHILDREN'S FEELINGS

Children may be consumed with thoughts and emotions that could benefit from a listening ear. Care providers can help children by reminding them that they are there to listen to them should they have any questions or thoughts they would like to talk about—the "good" stuff, the "bad" stuff, and the "I'm not so sure" stuff. Some children may want to speak about what is going on in their mind, and this invitation may present a welcoming opportunity to discuss and process the emotions they are experiencing. Other children may not want to openly discuss their emotions. These children should also be encouraged and supported to process their emotions in the ways that best work for them. Perhaps a game of basketball or painting a picture may be a more suitable approach of processing for some children. Ultimately, it is important that children know they have an adult in their life to whom they can go for advice or support. Although many care providers might like to have the answers to all of life's questions, sometimes a child's concerns may be outside their professional expertise. In situations such as these, care providers can connect children who are emotionally distressed and are unable to adequately cope with their day-to-day life with a therapist or counselor. Therapists have special skills and training to assist children who have difficulty processing their emotions and can be an excellent resource for children experiencing emotional distress. After all, a child can never have too many caring and supportive adults in their lives!

FROM THE HOW TO THE WHEN?

In this chapter we explored how entering foster care can impact a child's inner and interpersonal worlds. Questions pertaining to their role within a family unit and society will likely surface for children as they navigate their way in a new family environment. Children's identities may also be challenged as new environments impose change on their interpersonal roles. As a result, attending and tending to the inner worlds of children and making genuine efforts to invest in and nurture their inner and interpersonal worlds are essential. Assisting children in maintaining or establishing friendships can be helpful to their adjustment as they navigate their roles in the world. Furthermore, inviting, involving, and engaging children in decision-making and investing in their interests can demonstrate to children that their identities are meaningful and valued. For those children who align with a particular belief system (secular or non-secular), it may also be helpful for them to know there is an outlet for them to explore their beliefs, to ask questions, and to grow in a safe space where they can join in community with others who have similar values and beliefs. It is essential for children in foster care to know where and to whom they can go to ask questions, express themselves openly, and process their emotions. Children deserve to know there are adults in their lives who are able and willing to provide constant love and support. The provision of a safe, warm, and welcoming environment will promote healthier transitions and, ideally, healthier outcomes.

Before we delve into our next chapter, let's consider where we have ventured and where we are going. From a child's viewpoint, placement in foster care is often abrupt, frightening, and fraught with ambiguity. Children are removed from their homes, often with little or no forewarning and information, and are placed in a new residence with new people and new family dynamics. This whirlwind of activity and events can result in an inner and interpersonal shift that requires children to reconsider who they are, where they are, and where they are going. Although attempts can be made by care providers to ease children's fears, assure children they will be cared for, and affirm children's value, worth, and agency, there is one question that many children will silently long to have answered: "When can I go home?"

Why do I have to leave?
What is foster care?
Where are you taking me?
Who are these people?
How about ME?
WHEN CAN I GO HOME?

6

WHEN Can I Go Home?

CAN YOU RECALL a time in your life when someone you loved died and you replayed the last time you saw that person over and over again in your mind? Did you ever think, "I would do anything to just have that moment with him or her again?" Sadly, it is not uncommon for children in foster care to replay a similar scenario in their minds—the time when they will be reunited with loved ones from their original family. In this chapter, we will explore *temporal ambiguity* (i.e., a lack of clarity about the duration of the foster care placement; Mitchell, 2008; Mitchell & Kuczynski, 2010) and children's experiences of relationship losses as a result of being placed in foster care. Although not all children may desire to be reunited with their original family, the majority of children with whom I have spoken have indicated not only that they have yearned to be reconnected with their original parents and siblings, but also that they have suffered from chronic sorrow, complicated grief, and ambiguous loss (Boss, 1999) as a result of not knowing *if* and *when* they will ever return to being a "family" again.

HOW LONG WILL I BE IN FOSTER CARE?

Because foster care is not intended to be a permanent solution for a family in need of state support and resources, it is often impossible to advise children about the duration of their foster care placement. Most children desire to know when they can return home and often don't understand why a specific date or duration is not or cannot be provided to them. Unfortunately, the inability to provide children with this pertinent information can leave children feeling confused, frustrated, sad, and hopeless.

Craig's Experience
12 years old

Craig recalls the day he learned he would *never* return home, "They took me out to lunch at Burger King, and they told me that I was never allowed to go home again, so all of sudden I stopped eating and I said, 'Can I get this to go? I want to go home right now.' I didn't even go into the Play Park like I usually do because I was so sad."

Odelia's Experience
12 years old

Odelia was excited when she was first told she would be returning home. Unfortunately, her reunification date continues to be rescheduled. She explains, "And so when I found out [the reunification date] at the first court date, I was really happy. I was like, 'Yay, I'm going home!' and then they just kept remanding it, remanding it, remanding it. They just like do that all the time, and it hurt."

Brenda's Experience
11 years old

Brenda wonders if and when she is going to move again. She reports, "It felt kind of shocking and weird cause like, 'OK, this is like moving twice in like three days.' It's like three days later you move again. It's like, When is this gonna stop?"

Julia's Experience
15 years old

Julia recalls how she felt when she moved from one place to another, "I felt like a pinball . . . back and forth, back and forth."

As was noted by most of the children's reports, temporal ambiguity tended to surface as children's time in foster care progressed, and they had not yet returned home. Although these accounts were retroactive (i.e., children were reflecting on their experiences in the past 6 months to a year), it did appear as though children initially believed that their placement in foster care would be temporary (perhaps days or months) and were not expecting it to be long term. The definition and perception of "temporary" for an adult may vary greatly from how "temporary" is interpreted by a child.

HEALING SUGGESTION 6.1
C.A.R.E. FOR CHILDREN'S EXPERIENCES OF TEMPORAL AMBIGUITY

Unfortunately, most care providers do not know how long a child will be residing in foster care. Although a child's placement in foster care is intended to be temporary, children are often in foster care for anything but a "temporary" time. Children's perceptions of time vary, and it is important that they understand not only the meaning of foster care but also that the length of time they will be spending in foster care is dependent on many factors. Comments such as "Oh, don't worry, you won't be here long" or "This is just temporary, you'll be back with your mom soon" are not helpful to children when these statements are indeed not true. As Khadeja, age 20, advises, "What was not helpful to me was being told that it's only temporary, when you do not know how the situation will turn out." Being honest and open with children about the duration of foster care is important. It is also helpful for children to know that while they are in foster care, for whatever duration that may be, they will receive constant love and support from the adults in their lives.

I MISS MY FAMILY AND FRIENDS

The transition into foster care is fraught with loss. Children experience the loss of items of significance, schools, communities, friendships, and family members. Unlike losses due to death, many of the relational losses experienced by children in foster care are *ambiguous losses*. Ambiguous loss (Boss, 1999) refers to a lack of clarity about the psychological and/or physical presence of members of one's psychological family. A psychological family is the family, regardless of biological ties, that exists in one's mind (Boss, 2006). From my experiences, when children enter foster care they usually conceptualize their psychological family as their original family. It is important to note, however, that this psychological family often alters, and expands, as children navigate their way through the foster care system (Mitchell, in press).

Alicja's Experience
14 years old

Alicja reports, "It was like really sad and I didn't feel like I was welcomed home, and I didn't feel like I was like a part of that family. I felt like I was just a little kid that their parents died which my parents didn't die, but it felt like that, the way they were. So it was like pretty bad." Alicja's experience highlights the effects of ambiguous loss; her parents did not die but, when placed in foster care, she felt like she was a "kid that their parents died." Not only did she suffer from the loss of her parents, she no longer felt like she belonged to a family.

Craig's Experience
12 years old

Craig was heartbroken when he found out he could not return home to his mother. He shares, "I was like crying non-stop each day until I fell asleep during the day and my friends all wanted to play with me but then they figured out I was having a really sad moment so they stopped asking me if I was up or something. I was pretty much crying non-stop and every time I would get up, I would remember and start crying again."

Alicja's and Craig's reports capture children's experiences of the ambiguous loss of their parents—that is, having their parents psychologically present yet physically absent in their lives. Dominick and Alijca identify another type of ambiguous loss children can experience in foster care: the ambiguous loss of pets.

Dominick's Experience
9 years old

Dominick explains the loss of his pet and how he felt when he couldn't bring his cat with him to his foster home, "I was kind of sad because I was living with my mom, and my foster mom was allergic to cats so I couldn't bring [my cat]."

Alicja's Experience
14 years old

Alicja discusses how she felt when she lost the fish that was given to her as a birthday present by her parents. She shares, "I had a fish but when I went to a different foster house I didn't get the fish back. I only got the fish tank back and not the fishnet or the food or anything that I spent my life on, and it was like a birthday present for me. I was like 'Whaat?!' I was so upset cause that was my fish for my birthday, and I was like 'Oh my gosh!' . . . I'm not sure if they threw it in the toilet or they flushed it or they kept it. But like that got me, I was like, 'I wish I took it with me' 'cause it was like really sad, and I didn't know what happened to it. I would have thought that they would have wrote a note or say something about it . . . I was like, 'Oh my God. That's my fish,' and I was so sad. After that if anybody said fish or something like that, I was like 'waahh' and I would start crying because it was like hard. I hate eating fish, like I hate it. It's like ew, to hear fish and stuff, so it was like really sad."

These excerpts represent only a few of many ways children discussed experiencing ambiguous loss in their lives. Children often become preoccupied with the loss, wondering how their loved ones are doing, or what is happening or has happened to their loved ones. Unfortunately, one's preoccupation with the loss of a loved one in the absence of a means to consolidate the ambiguity can become a barrier to healing, resulting in immobilization (Boss, 2006). Boss states, "Disconnected from loved ones lost in mind or body . . . they are in a kind of limbo—blocked from coping or grieving, frozen in place, and thus brittle. Resiliency erodes" (p. 27).

Ambiguous loss of one's psychological family often leads to boundary ambiguity (Boss, 1999). In the previous chapter, we explored role ambiguity (i.e., a lack of clarity about one's role within an interpersonal context) and applied children's experiences of this type of ambiguity within a new familial context (e.g., a foster family or group home environment). In addition to experiencing role ambiguity within new familial contexts, children in foster care can experience role ambiguity within psychological family environments as well. This type of ambiguity, *boundary ambiguity*, refers to a lack of clarity about one's role within one's psychological family (Boss, 1999). Children not only may reflect on how their roles may change within a new family unit but also may consider how their roles within their (original) or psychological family have been impacted as a result of being placed in foster care.

Cheyenne's Experience
18 years old

Cheyenne reflects on the ambiguous loss she experienced when she entered foster care, "I really wondered why I can't visit with my niece or my nephew because I was their primary caregiver. I really wouldn't get a lot of sleep because I had to watch them and make sure they had everything done. It was just really hard for me to be separated from my niece and nephew because I had been with them for so long, and it was really hard to not have them around all the time and see like how they brightened my day. And it's just, I just felt so detached from them, and I never got to see them for 8 months. I would have liked to see the judge or my caseworker actually ask me, 'How can we make it a better situation, so that we can have you see your niece and nephew?' Because they never even knew that I was such a dominant figure in their lives. And they never asked me, so they never knew. And so, and I never got to go to court myself so I could advocate for myself, so I just would have liked to see somebody ask me about what part of our family I would have liked to see, because even though I didn't get along with my parents, um, there's other people in my family that I care a lot about."

Robert's Experience
20 years old

Robert's experience captures how children can be tormented by the ambiguous loss of their parents. He states, "Mentally I thought like, [my parents] were far away, but physically they were right around the corner from me and that kinda drove me insane for a while."

HEALING SUGGESTION 6.2
C.A.R.E. FOR CHILDREN'S EXPERIENCES OF AMBIGUOUS LOSS

Children in foster care commonly report experiences of ambiguous loss, yet these experiences are often left unacknowledged by adults within the foster care system (Lee & Whiting, 2007). Although the experience of ambiguous loss cannot be prevented for most children who are placed in foster care, there are ways to help children heal and find meaning amidst this ambiguity. Helping children in foster care learn how to find meaning and hope while experiencing ambiguous loss is an essential first step in the healing process (Boss, 2006) and building a relational home. Care providers can remind children that there is hope for their future, they have purpose in this world, and that, when applicable, multiple efforts are being made to reunite children with their family, even though it may take some time before this reunification may be possible. If a child is a ward of the court or a Crown ward and efforts are not being made to reunify the child with his or her original family, then hope can still be instilled in the child. Allowing and inviting children to discuss their concerns, fears, hopes, and dreams as they move forward in their lives in the physical absence of their loved ones is essential to the healing process. If a member of the child's psychological family is no longer able to visit with the child, helping the child to find ways to incorporate this person into his or her life symbolically can also assist the healing process. Later in this chapter, I will address the various strategies used by children in foster care to cope with ambiguous loss. In her book *Loss, Trauma, and Resilience*, Boss (2006) discusses multiple ways to assist individuals who are experiencing ambiguous loss. Care providers who are interested in learning more about this specific type of ambiguity are encouraged to refer to this resource for additional insights into finding meaning and hope amidst ambiguous loss.

WHEN AND HOW OFTEN DO I GET TO SEE MY FAMILY?

When placed in foster care, children may begin to wonder when they will be able to see their loved ones again. Children who do not have a clear understanding of the foster care system (i.e., structural ambiguity) may also wonder *if* they will ever see their family again. Take a moment to consider someone in your life whom you hold near and dear to your heart. The thought of this person brings you joy, happiness, warmth, and peace. Within moments, however, you find yourself separated from this individual and are told you may never see him or her again. "Never?" you think to yourself. That's a long time. Sadness, fear, desperation, and hopelessness set in.

Even though adults may not say the words "never" or "forever," when children are separated from a loved one and they are not permitted to see this person, it can feel like "never" or "forever." Being separated from someone you love with no means to communicate or express yourself can be a dreadful experience. Children's reports capture this experience:

Craig's Experience
12 years old

When Craig was informed that he was never allowed to go home again, he spent days "crying non-stop." Craig did not understand why he was never allowed to return home. It wasn't until he called his mother that he learned that "never" actually meant only 6 more years. Craig states, "I was still in tears when I called my mom, and she knew I was crying, like when I called her, and I said, 'Why am I never allowed to come home again?' and she said, 'No, they got it all wrong,' I was allowed to come home when I was 18 instead of 16. I was pretty mad at my workers about that."

Denise's Experience
13 years old

Denise explains her experience of ambiguous loss, as well as how difficult it is for her to witness her sister suffer from ambiguous loss and structural ambiguity. She states, "I got tooken away from my mom. That was really hard. Really harsh ... I just moved into my foster house, and I was crying for my mom and stuff ... I haven't been allowed [to talk to my mom] for 3 months now. The only thing that bugs me is that [my sister] says, "I miss mommy a lot" so that's what bugs me and then I start crying. She said that to me at school once. 'Yes, I know. I do too.' And I started crying and everyone started crying, 'What's wrong? What's wrong?' like 'Holy Geeze. Nothing.' ... I try to tell her to stop saying it. Yeah, I know she's young. She really doesn't understand or anything, but somewhat I think she knows what is going on, but then again, I don't know if she knows what's going on."

Mark's Experience
13 years old

Mark is confused about why he can't have visits with his mother. He states, "I don't even have visits with [my mom]. She can go over and see my sister at my uncle's but why can't I go and see her and stuff? It's weird. I have no idea [why that is]."

The experiences of Denise and Mark are filled with ambiguous and symbolic significance, portraying elements of structural ambiguity, ambiguous loss, and threats to a child's connection to his or her psychological family. Restricting children's access to people of importance to them and/or information related to their visitation rights can elicit stressful appraisals and contribute to further psychological trauma. It is important that children are given an opportunity to discuss their feelings about their losses and separations and that they be provided with ample information about their visitation rights.

When asked about their family visitations, children's reports suggest that they want attention paid to their personal time with their parents and siblings, the length of the visitations, and the opportunity for additional visitations when needed.

Jessica's Experience
12 years old

Jessica reports that she and her siblings all visit with her mom together. She states, "We have our little visits with all of us with her," but Jessica would also like to see her mom on her own.

Odelia's Experience
12 years old

Odelia also mentions that she would like some one-on-one time with her mother and that, sometimes, her sibling prevents that from occurring. She shares, "I love my mom. She gives me a lot more attention now that I've confronted her and stuff, and she gives me like, equal attention. But my brother . . . he often comes to my mom's when I'm on my visit with her, just me and my mom and he's interrupting on that. Sometimes I don't like it, and sometimes I'm OK with it. I like to see my brother and stuff, but sometimes I just wanna be like me and mom, that's our visit time."

Donnie's Experience
12 years old

Donnie discusses how his visits with his mom have declined. He used to see her often but "now she only sees me once a month. It kind of sucks." Donnie would prefer to see his mom more often.

HEALING SUGGESTION 6.3
C.A.R.E. FOR FAMILY VISITATIONS

Care providers can communicate to children that visitations can be made with their loved ones and can explain the nature of the visits (i.e., who will be in attendance, how long the visits will last, where the visits will be held, the purpose of the visits, and so forth). If visits with certain individuals are not in the best interest of the child, then this information should also be communicated to the child. Being honest and providing information in an age-appropriate manner can be helpful approaches as children will be less prone to self-blame and/or other incorrect beliefs. Attention can also be paid to how often children are able to visit with their original family and friends and the quality of the visitations. Sometimes children will want "alone" time with their parents and/or siblings. If it is possible to consider and arrange for these different types of visitations, this can be particularly helpful to children who are coping with the loss of their family members. As illustrated by the children's reports throughout this book, a physical death is not the only type of separation that evokes loss and grief. Ambiguous loss can be just as traumatic for children who are trying to navigate their way in the foster care system in the physical absence of their loved ones.

WHAT CAN I DO TO COPE WITH EXPERIENCES OF LOSS?

There is no doubt that the majority of children in foster care are experiencing some type of loss and are faced with deciding how they will cope with these experiences. Coping is defined as "constantly changing cognitive and behavioral efforts to manage specific external and/or internal demands that are appraised as taxing or exceeding the resources of the person" (Lazarus & Folkman, 1984, p. 141). That is, coping is the way children manage stressful demands and impositions on their inner and interpersonal worlds, including those that impose on their relationships with loves ones. Every child will have his or her unique way of expressing his or her emotions and coping with stressful life events; some children may internalize their emotions, whereas others may outwardly express them in words or behaviors. How children cope with stress and loss will depend on their interpretation and the context of the situation. As children illustrate in their reports on coping strategies, an individual's coping strategy is dynamic, multidimensional, and flexible to change across situations.

Angela's Experience
12 years old

Angela equates her experience of being in foster care to an actor in a play. She states, "I don't know, I felt like, you know how Shakespeare says, 'We are all mere players in, like, we are all like a play and we're just acting out.' It felt like I was being played, like told a script and I had no choice but to not change it or just go with what I was told. I was told what to say and how to say it and end of story sort of thing." Angela reports that she has never spoken to anyone about how she was feeling at the time, nor would she have liked to talk about it. She kept how she felt to herself then, and she still does.

Denise's Experience
13 years old

Denise confides, "I still miss my mom. [The Department of Social Services] wouldn't let me talk to my mom for two weeks." When asked how she dealt with this experience, she replies, "I think I went outside and hung out by myself."

As illustrated in the reports by Angela and Denise, some children chose to cope with their emotions by internalizing their emotions and spending time alone. Children who do not have individuals with whom they can speak about their loss can suppress their emotions and become overwhelmed with grief, resulting in poor adjustment (DeSpelder & Strickland, 2010). What is interesting to note is that although children, such as Angela, indicated that they never really spoke to anyone about their feelings, these children were very open and willing to share their feelings and opinions with the interviewer. It is hopeful and quite possible, then, that children will express their feelings should there be an adult who is welcoming, warm, and willing to listen to them.

In addition to internalizing their feelings, another coping strategy reported by children was finding something to do to occupy themselves, such as listening to music or engaging in an activity.

Gabriella's Experience
12 years old

Gabriella discusses how activities can help children cope with their stress. She states, "If you do stuff it gets your stress off and things. I usually play outside or go up to my room and listen to music. I like to play basketball, floor hockey, riding my bikes."

Odelia's Experience
12 years old

Odelia reports, "I just kinda lay there, sometimes on my bed and maybe like play a game, or something. Take my mind off of it a bit."

Mark's Experience
13 years old

Mark also believes that activities can be helpful to cope with one's stress. He talks about the thoughts that resurface in his head and how sports have been a useful coping strategy for him. He explains, "It's like I still get really mad about that stuff. It's like I'm sitting in class or something, and it still comes into my head. All of the things that happened. [I talked to] the counselor. But it didn't, it doesn't help for some reason. I don't know why . . .I'm just trying to do lots of like stuff to get rid of it, you know. Like sports and all of the fun stuff that can take my mind off of it all the time. And like it's gone down a lot over time, so it will go down."

Derrick's Advice
13 years old

Derrick also believes that keeping occupied can be helpful to children who are stressed and worried about their families. He advises, "Watch movies and stuff to keep you occupied. Or play video games because if you listen to music then it's just gonna make you think more about foster care. Like it still does sometimes. Bring a stereo so that at nighttime it's easy to go to sleep because you worry about your family."

These children's experiences demonstrate that, *at times*, some children may prefer engaging in activities rather than talking about how they are feeling. I emphasize "at times" because children do not have only *one* strategy that they use to cope with stressful events. It is possible that some children may have a preferred coping strategy; however, it is also quite probable that every new stressful event has the potential to evoke its own coping response and, furthermore, children may choose alternate strategies to cope with the same event. A one-size fits all approach cannot and should not be applied to children and how they cope with and grieve their losses.

Some children reported that problem-solving, including running away as a means to solve the predicament in which they found themselves (i.e., being placed in foster care), were ways they chose to respond to the losses they experienced.

Donnie's Experience
12 years old

Donnie discusses the efforts he made to reunite himself with his mother. He reports, "Well, my first foster house I went to was in the same city, like five minutes away, and [within an hour of being placed there] I ran away and went home. Then the [foster parent] picked me up and brought me back. He drove me back to the foster house. My mom was kind of disappointed. I said, 'It's OK. At least I'm here.'"

Craig's Experience
12 years old

Craig also decided to run away from his foster care placement so he could see his mom. He shares, "One day I got so mad that I quickly got on my rollerblades and ran away and went to mom's house because she lived on the other side of [the city], and I knew how to get there. I got there really, really late at night and [my foster mom] had just called her by the time I was just about there because she couldn't get a hold of my mom until later on when she kept calling. Then right when I was on my mom's street, my [foster mom] pulled up in her car, and she honked and rolled down her window really fast and said, 'Stay there' and she came on the driveway behind me, and she turned around, and then she picked me up and took me back to my foster home. She said that I just had to stay [at my foster home] and not run away and stuff like that. If I wanted to see [my mom], just call her or set up another visit to go and see her, or whatever."

The experiences shared by Donnie and Craig illustrate how running away from one's home can be viewed as a suitable and viable option to responding to their losses and other stressful situations. Fortunately, all of these children were located and were returned to their placements/homes safely; however, this positive outcome is not the case for all children. It is important to consider that running away, a potentially dangerous strategy, can be used by children to cope with the challenges imposed on their inner and interpersonal worlds. Providing children with an opportunity to discuss their feelings, brainstorm healthy and safe ways to address their feelings, and other safe outlets to reconnect with their psychological family (physically or symbolically) can be helpful approaches to use with children who consider running away from their homes as a means to an end.

Other children discussed how seeking out the company of others was a means to cope with ambiguous loss.

Denise's Experience
13 years old

Denise recalls, "I could hang out with people; try to get to know people and stuff. I got to know a bit of people, like starting to make some friends and stuff. [It was helpful] a little bit but I still miss my mom."

Christina's Advice
11 years old

Christina offers care providers advice about how to help children stay connected with friends who may be far away. She suggests, "If [children] have a cell phone, they might want to get some minutes on it so they can text their friends and stuff. Like if they didn't want to talk on the phone, they'd be able to text messages to them and stuff." Christina's advice also draws attention to the possibility that some children may not feel like talking when they are grieving. Providing children with a cell phone, or minutes for their cell phone, can create opportunities for them to communicate in way that meets their needs (e.g., writing or speaking).

Some children discussed how engaging in activities that memorialized their families were helpful strategies to cope with loss and grief. Children's reports illustrate that activities or rituals that remind them of their psychological family offer them comfort.

Gabriella's Experience
12 years old

Gabriella explains that "after my social worker told me I wasn't going to go home for a while, then I got mad and upset and stuff and scared." When asked if there was anything that helped her during this time, Gabriella replies, "Well I brought my um, there's this [favorite toy of mine]. Oh, and there's, there's tigers, monkeys, ahh, a spotted cheetah, I think. And yeah, my parents bought me a chimpanzee, and I brought that with me [and it made me feel better]."

Alicja's Experience
14 years old

Alicja reflects on feeling "really sad" when she entered foster care because she missed her parents. When asked if there was anything that she did or had in her life that made her feel better during this time, she responds, "A picture of my dad." As mentioned in Chapter 1, caring for children's personal belongings of significance during their entry into foster care can be helpful not only during the home transfer but also during their experiences of grief and loss.

Denise's Experience
13 years old

Denise believes that communicating one's thoughts on paper to the [ambiguously deceased] person can be helpful to children who are grieving. She states, "[When I miss my mom] I write her a letter. You should see how many letters I write her."

As demonstrated by these children's reports, loss can evoke multiple coping and grieving responses; the internalizing of emotions, the desire to partake in activities, the search for a resolution, running away or toward one's loss, seeking out the company of friends or pets, and memorializing family are just a few of many strategies used by children. It is essential that caregivers C.A.R.E. for these losses, as children's grief is often disenfranchised and ignored. Assisting children by encouraging them to address their feelings of loss (in whatever way that may be), supporting them in exploring their feelings as they arise, and nurturing them as they grieve over the loss of their loved ones are essential to the healing process.

HEALING SUGGESTION 6.4
C.A.R.E. FOR CHILDREN'S HEALING AND COPING PROCESSES

Many children will need encouragement, support, and nurturing to assist them in coping with ambiguous loss. "The psychological family is an essential part of rediscovering hope. After a massive and confusing disaster, a person's psychological family may be the only thing familiar, and no one can take it away. This psychological connection to family, when all else is lost, becomes a resource for discovering hope again" (Boss, 2006, p. 195). There are a variety of ways that children can maintain connections with their loved ones. Some children may like to write in a journal, create a scrapbook of their loved ones, listen to music, or cuddle a stuffed animal that reminds them of their psychological family, or engage in a sport or activity that they played with their loved ones. The opportunity for children to have a space to engage in personal and social rituals and express their love and affection for the physically absent individuals can be helpful to the healing process (DeSpelder & Strickland, 2010).

Individuals, regardless of their age, may behave or act like frightened children when they experience a significant loss (Despelder & Strickland, 2010). These authors offer the following advice for supporters of individuals who are experiencing grief: "A hug may be more comforting than words. Having someone who can 'simply listen' can be helpful. The key to being a good listener is to refrain from making judgments about whether the feelings expressed by a bereaved person are 'right' or 'wrong,' 'good' or 'bad.' The emotions and thoughts evoked by loss may not be expected, but they can be appropriate and valid within a [child's] experience" (Despelder & Strickland, p. 343).

Ultimately, each child in foster care deserves to be understood, appreciated, supported, and encouraged to cope with the losses they experience. By attending to children's experiences of loss, grief, and ambiguity, care providers demonstrate to children that feelings of loss and grief are natural, that there is value in expressing their feelings (verbally or nonverbally), and that there are ways to C.A.R.E. for children's healing and coping processes.

WILL THINGS GET EASIER WITH TIME?

Many children identified time as being a contributing factor for adjustment to the placement in foster care. For example, Julia (15 years old) advises, "It really sucks. It gets easier with time." Although the initial placement into foster care was perceived as stressful, children's reports suggest that with time these stressful appraisals would be reappraised more positively.

Christina's Experience
11 years old

Christina offers the following advice to children who have recently entered the foster care system: "Usually what people have always told me is that things have to get worse before they can get better. You might not necessarily like it but it will work out for the best, hopefully."

Dominick's Advice
9 years old

Dominick also advises that time can be a supportive resource. He states, "Like try to get used to it and then first see how your parents are like and, first you cannot be nice and then try to get, once you get used to it, you'll get better and better in your foster house."

Jazmine's Advice

18 years old

Jazmine reflects on how her life in foster care got easier with time. She shares, "Being in different and a lot of foster homes was really like hard for me. When I was [younger], I came down with the sickness and I was in the hospital for about a month because of it. It was very difficult, and I was depressed. When I moved to [a group home a few years later] it was still kinda hard to begin, but when I turned 16, it's when things started to get easier, and then I started actually doing good in school, you know, going to college. I was the first one to graduate high school and go to college in my family, so it was a good thing. So, but at a younger age, things were not easy at all, and I feel like things should have been easy at a younger age, and then got harder as I got older. But it was very much the opposite."

HEALING SUGGESTION 6.5

C.A.R.E. FOR THE HEALING PROPERTIES OF TIME

There is an old saying, "Time heals all wounds." Although I would not venture to say that all children, or adults for that matter, completely heal from their wounds, I do believe time has a magical way of transforming our pain and helping us to better cope and heal from the experiences that have caused the wounding. Being patient with children, allowing them time to process, respecting their need for space, and providing opportunities for them to explore and discuss their feelings throughout time can be invaluable to their growth and healing.

ANSWERING THE WHY, WHAT, WHERE, WHO, HOW, AND WHEN

As we have journeyed together and explored children's experiences as they transition into foster care, the questions that children ask of us illustrate the importance of not just hearing their questions but genuinely and actively listening to children's concerns, fears, and suggestions for meaningful change. In this chapter, we explored children's experiences of temporal ambiguity and ambiguous loss. We listened as children told us about missing their loved ones, coping with their grief, and advice they have to offer to other children in foster care who are missing family members and friends. We bear witness to how the transition into foster care can leave children confused, afraid, uncertain, and distressed about their past, their present, and their future.

Ultimately, if we listen carefully, we can hear the voices of children's hearts. By creatively mastering the art of asking questions, children invite us to consider how experiences of loss and ambiguity shatter their world and how to build a relational home where they can feel safe and answers can arise. Where might one find such a space? As we travel into the final chapter of our journey, we arrive at our final destination: the place where healing resides.

7

Building a Relational Home for Children's Experiences of Loss, Ambiguity, and Trauma in Foster Care

ANSWERING THE WHY? WHAT? WHERE? WHO? HOW? WHEN?

Why do I have to leave?
    What is foster care?
        Where are you taking me?
            Who are these people?
                How about me?
                    When can I go home?
                        Can you hear me?
                            Are you there?

As we have journeyed together and listened to children's courageous stories about loss, ambiguity, grief, and trauma in foster care, their voices alert us to the need for change, the need for enfranchisement, and the need to truly be heard. It is my hope that the healing suggestions in this book, inspired by the children themselves, will provide a foundation to build a relational home for children entering care. Physical health and safety, shelter, permanency, and education are often the primary focus of well-being for children in foster care, likely because these needs are easier to identify and measure than children's emotional and relational needs, which are often overlooked. The experiences of children, offered in this book, give voice to their need for a relational home where their thoughts and emotions can be cared for and nurtured.

Do you recall a time in your life when you felt afraid and completely alone? If you have experienced such a time, try to remember what it was like to feel such despair. Perhaps you felt disconnected from the world, misunderstood, insignificant, or hopeless. Now imagine what it would feel like to harbor these thoughts in your mind and feelings in your heart without anyone to console you. As illustrated throughout this book, children in foster care often feel that their questions are left unanswered and their experiences of loss and ambiguity are unacknowledged and unattended. Fortunately, care providers have the resources and healing power to change this reality. We can invest in understanding children's experiences from their perspectives in an effort to walk with them on their journey and provide a relational home as they navigate their way in foster care.

How do we build a relational home for our children? Let's travel back and reflect on children's experiences and advice during our journey with them. What have the voices of children inspired in us? Whether you have learned something new, have been reminded of something that you had forgotten, or have received affirmation of something you know, we are encouraged to consider what it is that we can do to answer the questions that children greet us with as we walk alongside them on their journey. Throughout this book, we have explored children's experiences of placement reason ambiguity (i.e., a lack of clarity about the reason for being placed into foster care), structural ambiguity (i.e., a lack of clarity about the meaning of foster care), placement context ambiguity (i.e., a lack of clarity about the context of the foster home), temporal ambiguity (i.e., a lack of clarity about the duration of the foster care placement), relationship ambiguity (i.e., a lack of clarity about the people with whom they will be placed), role ambiguity (i.e., a lack of clarity about one's role within familial contexts), and ambiguous loss (i.e., a lack of clarity about the psychological and/or physical presence of members of their psychological family).

We have listened to children's experiences of loss and disenfranchised grief and to children's advice about best practices to assist them as they navigate their way into and through the foster care system. Thanks to the courageous sharing of their voices, we can listen actively and consider how to facilitate more effective and meaningful practices to meet children's needs. Healing suggestions have been offered throughout the book to identify ways to minimize children's experiences of ambiguity, to recognize and acknowledge experiences of loss and grief, and to support children as their assumptive worlds shatter and they navigate their way into and through the world of foster care. A complete list of the healing suggestions and a respective C.A.R.E. checklist can be found in Appendix C. By applying the healing suggestions offered throughout this book, it is hoped that care providers will build a healing sanctuary where children's fears, thoughts, questions, and dreams are welcomed, acknowledged, and nurtured.

As our journey comes to a close and we consider best practices to build a relational home, I would like to take a moment to draw attention to and reflect upon a special ingredient that deserves emphasis here: that is, the celebration of a child's presence in the world. To help paint a more vivid picture of the importance of celebrating a child's life, in this case a birthday, I would like to offer the following story:

In my current position I facilitate a state youth advisory panel of young adults with foster care experience who range in age from 17 to 23 years. One of the traditions that I have intentionally created for our team is the celebration of members' birthdays. I can recall the following event like it was yesterday. One of our members was turning 20 years old, and we were excited to surprise him with a birthday cake. Shortly after he blew out his candles, he looked at us with tears in his eyes and said, "Wow, y'all, you know this is my first birthday cake." It was the first birthday cake he had received in his 20 years of being alive. He shared that he had always dreamed of having a birthday celebration. In other words, no one had ever provided him with a celebration to honor the day he was born and graced this world.

I share this story in an effort to illustrate how the lives of children can be impacted when they witness their life as meaningful and significant to others. Unfortunately, far too many children, and adults for that matter, have said to me, "This is the first time someone has acknowledged my birthday." Because one's life is so valuable, precious, and meaningful, it is disheartening to hear such stories. While it is possible for some children to be raised within a family where birthdays are not to be celebrated, it is important for children to believe that their existence is a cause for celebration. Celebrating a child's worth can appear in many forms: a celebration of children's accomplishments, personal growth, birthdays, or any other joys they experience. It may involve a birthday party, a special meal with family or friends, or simply telling children, "I am so glad you are in this world." Children's accomplishments, successes, trials, and efforts also deserve continuous acknowledgment and affirmation. Ultimately, building a relational home is more than providing a space for children to grieve and express their emotions. It is also a place where children can dream, hope, and celebrate their wonderful, unique contribution to the world by simply being alive. A relational home is one that creates a space for tears, for fears, for love, and for healing.

Although this book is primarily focused on a child's journey into foster care, it is important to emphasize that a relational home should be available to children throughout their time in foster care. Children need to know that they will have a relational home that is sustainable, particularly for their grief, during the onset of their loss as well as weeks, months, and years later (DeSpelder & Strickland, 2010).

Ultimately, children in foster care deserve to have their voices heard, to be provided with a safe space to express their emotions, and to believe that there are people in their lives who will support, encourage, and love them unconditionally.

To receive unconditional love from others is valuable indeed; however, children must also learn how to practice the unconditional love of oneself. Children can build, nurture, and heal the relational home within themselves when they are taught and experience the affirmation of their own innate worth, competence, purpose, and value in life. From my own interactions with children, youth, and young adults in foster care, I have learned that many of them, regardless of age, struggle with building this home within themselves. As a means to assist worthy, competent, purposeful, and valued builders, I offer a list of daily affirmations that children of all ages can read to inspire and celebrate their worth and uniqueness in the world (see Appendix D). In order for a relational home to be sustainable, it is essential for a child's inner and interpersonal world to fill with unconditional love.

In addition to the healing suggestions in this book, there are many educational resources available to care providers who care for children who are experiencing trauma and loss. For example, the National Child Traumatic Stress Network (www.nctsn.org) has information about trauma, traumatic events, and traumatic stress in childhood, as well as suggestions on how to assist traumatized children. Similarly, the National Alliance for Grieving Children (http://www.nationalallianceforgrievingchildren.org/) is an excellent resource to learn more about childhood grief, bereavement camps, local and national support, and additional resources for children who are grieving. The Child Welfare League of America (www.cwla.org) provides child welfare resources and training to assist care providers in their efforts to ensure the safety, permanency, and well-being of children in foster care. The International Foster Care Organization (www.ifco.info) also provides a forum for members of the international foster care community to network with one another to promote and support family-based foster care worldwide. Ultimately, by familiarizing oneself with the resources and partners available to support children and care providers involved in the foster care system, a relational home is built not only for the children, but also for the caring adults in a child's life who need and deserve a healing sanctuary to be welcomed, acknowledged, and heard as well.

In closing, I thank you for participating in this journey and for the time you have taken to listen, consider, and acknowledge the experiences of loss and ambiguity that children experience when they are removed from their homes, separated from their families, enter a system with which they are unfamiliar, placed in homes with people whom they do not know, plagued with questions and events that challenge their inner and interpersonal worlds, and, amidst it all, strive to overcome the ambiguity and grief they experience as a result of multiple significant losses and transformative change.

It is my hope that by journeying alongside our children, we have not only considered, but also empathically experienced the transition into foster care from a child's frame of reference. By acknowledging and attending to children's experiences of loss, ambiguity, grief, and trauma, a relational home can be built to nurture child well-being and foster healing. Ultimately, by enfranchising this neglected life transition, children learn that there is meaning in experience; that the foster care system is intended to be a safe haven to protect them from harm; that the adults placed in their lives in foster care are there to C.A.R.E. and provide them with comfort, acceptance, and love; that new people will come into their lives whom they can trust, depend upon, and love; that they are masters of their own destiny; and that time, along with those inner and interpersonal experiences that occur during this continuum, can bring with it transformational properties to reconstruct one's assumptive world and create a journey of hope, love, and healing.

Thank you for listening.

Thank you for caring.

Appendix A

A VALUE MODEL OF C.A.R.E.: A BLUEPRINT FOR BUILDING
A RELATIONAL HOME

E	VALUE ACTION	VALUE STATEMENT
ᴄATE	Actively listen, provide information, and ask and answer questions, appropriately, when needed.	"Your communication to me about your needs[1], experiences,[2] and aspirations is important and valued."
AFFIRM	Affirm a child's strengths, potential, and worthiness of unconditional love.	"You are important and valued."
RECOGNIZE	Recognize and acknowledge the needs, experiences, and aspirations that are significant to a child.	"Recognizing and acknowledging your needs, experiences, and aspirations are important and valued."
ENSURE	Attend to a child's needs to ensure that his or her safety, permanency, and well-being are met.	"Attending to and ensuring that your needs are met, are important and valued."

[1] Needs are defined as emotional, physical, social, environmental, intellectual, and spiritual needs.

[2]The scope of this book focuses specifically on the experiences of loss and ambiguity during the transition into foster care.

Appendix B

A PHENOMENOLOGICAL JOURNEY: PHILOSOPHICAL
AND METHODOLOGICAL CONSIDERATIONS

The majority of children's reports presented in this book were retrieved from the *Transitioning into Foster Care* project, which was a 4-year dissertation research study. The following information provides a brief overview of the guiding philosophy and theoretical frameworks, lines of inquiry, methods, and analytic procedure of the study.

GUIDING PHILOSOPHY AND THEORETICAL FRAMEWORKS

The study's philosophical and theoretical frameworks focus on understanding lived experience from the perspective of the individuals who are directly experiencing the phenomenon under investigation. Hermeneutic phenomenology, introduced by Heidegger, is interested in how human beings ascribe meaning, significance, and value to things (Benner, 1994). Similarly, cognitive appraisal theory (Lazarus & Folkman, 1984) focuses on how individuals appraise transactions that threaten matters of significance and value to the individuals. How people interpret a transaction will be influenced by their culture, beliefs, and past experiences. Hermeneutic phenomenological analysis was considered to be helpful as the study's guiding philosophy because it enabled me to examine and interpret potentially diverse beliefs and evaluations of the phenomenon under investigation (in this case, children's lived experience of the transition into foster care).

An exhaustive description of cognitive appraisal theory will not be attempted in this section; however, I will provide a brief summary of the theoretical framework for those readers who are interested in the theory guiding this work. Cognitive appraisal theory (Lazarus & Folkman, 1984), which originated from stress and coping research, focuses on how individuals appraise (i.e., evaluate) transactions that occur between themselves and their environment. Similar to the philosophy of hermeneutic phenomenology, the emphasis is placed on the *individual's interpretation* of the transaction and not on a shared understanding or multiple perspectives of any given transaction. Therefore, in this study (and in this book), children's appraisals of the transactions resulting from the transition into foster care (i.e., foster care transition transactions; Mitchell, 2008; Mitchell & Kuczynski, 2010) are considered the primary source of information for dissemination, and other parties' perceptions of these transactions are not the focus of analysis. Although this approach may be considered a limitation by researchers informed by other frameworks (e.g., social constructionism, attachment theory, etc.), attending to the perceptions of a specific population is not viewed as a limitation within a hermeneutic phenomenological framework. Hermeneutic phenomenological studies are not designed to prove whether a participant's interpretation of a situation is justified by others involved in the transaction; rather, self-interpretations are respected and honored. Individuals' appraisals and interpretation are believed to reflect their subjective realities, and it is these realities that are explored and discussed.

Cognitive appraisal theory asserts that individuals have two main appraisal processes: primary and secondary appraisals. When an event occurs, individuals first evaluate the event (i.e., the primary appraisal) to determine whether the event will impose upon their personal beliefs, values, and commitments. The resulting appraisal will be benign-positive (i.e., the individual appraises the event to result in a positive outcome), irrelevant (i.e., the individual appraises the event will have no effect on his or her beliefs, values, and commitments), or a stress appraisal (i.e., the individual appraises the event to harm, threaten, or challenge his or her personal beliefs, values, and commitments, with a potential for a negative outcome). It is the latter appraisal (i.e., a stress appraisal) that can simultaneously induce secondary appraisals (i.e., an individual's evaluation of what can or might be done to manage a stressful transaction). This usually involves an evaluation of the resources present in an individual's life and each resource's potential availability, accessibility, and effectiveness in coping with the stressful transaction. Therefore, cognitive appraisal theory was selected as a guiding framework to explore how children interpret and appraise the events (e.g., removal from one's home, placement into a new residence, etc.) that occur within transactions that transpire as a result of their being placed in the foster care system.

ADDITIONAL GUIDING THEORIES

In addition to cognitive appraisal theory, the theories of the assumptive world (Janoff-Bulman, 1989; Kaufmann, 2002; Parkes, 1971), ambiguous loss (Boss, 1999), and disenfranchised grief (Doka, 1989) contributed greatly to my exploration of how children's lives are impacted as a result of being removed from their families and placed in the child welfare system.

The assumptive world refers to the "assumptions or beliefs that ground, secure, or orient people, that give a sense of reality, meaning, or purpose to life" (Kaufmann, 2002, p. 1). In other words, the assumptive world is a conceptual system that is founded on people's expectations about the world and themselves (Janoff-Bulman, 1989). When significant change occurs in an individual's life, it can disrupt or challenge an individual's assumptive world; that is, an individual's beliefs can be challenged, changed, and transformed (Parkes, 1971). In the case of change in the assumptive world, this change can often be traumatic (Kauffman, 2002). Furthermore, where there is change, there is always loss. Where there is loss, there is a space for healing.

When children are placed in foster care, their assumptive world shatters. They are removed from their homes and are often separated from loved ones. Most times, these separations result in a child's experience of ambiguous loss—that is, a loss that involves someone who is psychologically present but physically absent, or someone who is physically present but psychologically absent. For example, although their original family members may no longer be physically present in their lives (i.e., living in their new homes or engaging in physical transactions on a daily basis), these loved ones may be very present in children's minds. Because of this, it is important to acknowledge how these types of losses can impact a child's life.

Boss (2006) asserts that "ambiguous loss is inherently traumatic because the inability to resolve the situation causes pain, confusion, shock, distress, and often immobilization. Without closure, the trauma of this unique kind of loss becomes chronic" (p. 4). As such, the theory of ambiguous loss has meaningfully guided my interpretations of children's experiences of foster care transition transactions and how children make meaning of the losses they experience. Unfortunately, as is becoming more and more apparent in my research, experiences of ambiguous loss and symbolic loss within the foster care system are often disenfranchised.

Doka's (1989) theory of disenfranchised grief has been of great assistance to me in interpreting how children's losses are disenfranchised in the foster care system. That is, children's experiences of ambiguous loss and symbolic losses often are not acknowledged, children experience losses that are not recognized in society as significant (e.g., loss of non-kin siblings, case managers, etc.), and children can be excluded as grievers (i.e., there is little to no social recognition of their need to grieve and mourn their losses). I have made reference to children's experiences of disenfranchised grief in this book based on the experiences shared by children in the interviews when they were not directly asked about their grief. In other words, this research study on children's experiences of the transition into foster care focused on children's appraisals of transactions resulting from the transition into foster care and the events that could induce ambiguous interpretations. The design invited children to lead the conversation and its direction in relation to the experiences they deemed important. Therefore, when I first began exploring this phenomenon, the guiding inquiries were focused mostly on experiences of ambiguity and not specifically on their losses, although this information did spontaneously emerge in their reports. Because loss, which was not a primary line of inquiry, emerged as a prominent theme from the data, it signaled to me the need to develop a study that focused explicitly on children's experiences of loss in foster care. Accordingly, my current research examines youth's experiences of loss, grief, and disenfranchisement while in the foster care system. These findings will be shared in future publications.

LINES OF INQUIRY

The following lines of inquiry guided this study's inquiry process:
How do children interpret the transition into foster care?

1. To what extent are children's interpretations of experiences related to the foster care transition understood in terms of the construct of ambiguity? For instance, do

children experience a lack of clarity about certain experiences and/or events during the transition into foster care?

2. What transactions emerge from the transition into foster care, and how do children appraise and experience these transactions?

STUDY SAMPLE

Twenty children, 8 to 15 years-old, from a Children's Aid Society agency in a central province in Canada participated in the study. The agency was located in a mid-sized city with close proximity to rural communities. Visible minorities represent about 10% of the population. The total number of participants in the sample was based on the sample principle of representativeness (Patterson & Williams, 2002); therefore, all children at the agency who met the study criteria were invited to participate in the study. The participants had been in foster care for a minimum of 6 months to a maximum of 3 years. The average age of the sample was 12 years old, the average time spent in care was 20 months, and, on average, children had two placements within 3 years of being in care.

Four criteria were required for participant eligibility in the study: (1) foster care status—regular foster care; (2) age—8 to 15 years old (3) duration in foster care—more than 6 months and less than 3 years, and (4) placement type—non-kinship foster care.

Criteria 1

Because participants were required to partake in a group workshop and discuss potentially sensitive matters during a personal interview, only children in regular foster care were invited to participate in the study. Therefore children in specialized and treatment foster care, who usually fall within the clinical range for externalizing and internalizing behaviors, were not part of the sample.

Criteria 2

Children who participated in this study required sufficient language abilities to verbally communicate how they experienced the transition into foster care. Therefore, children in the concrete operational (i.e., 8 to 11 years old) and formal operational (i.e., 12 to 15 years of age) stages of cognitive development were invited to participate in this study. Children under the age of 8 were not recruited to participate.

Criteria 3

Experiencing parental and sibling loss and transitioning into foster care can be a traumatic experience. As such, it was decided that children are extremely vulnerable during the transition into foster care and it may not be in their best interest to be interviewed immediately upon entrance into care. Therefore, children who had been in care for less than 6 months were not eligible to participate in the study. This criteria was also established because research has shown that the majority of children who experience parental loss do not acknowledge the loss until at least 6 months after the incident (Worden, 2005). This being said, the study's findings suggest that children may acknowledge the loss prior to 6 months, but their ability to process and discuss how this experience has affected them may not happen immediately. Ultimately, asking children about their experiences of loss should be treated with care, consideration, and understanding.

Criteria 4

Because ambiguity was the main construct of inquiry, it was assumed that children entering placements with care providers who are strangers (i.e., non-kinship care) may provide more insight into ambiguous experiences than would children who are placed with care providers with whom they may be familiar (i.e., kinship foster care). In the final sample, all but one of the participants had been placed into a non-kinship home upon entrance into foster care. It was found later in the data collection that one child had initially been placed in a kinship home but was preparing to transition into a non-kinship home placement. Because her interview focused on her experiences of ambiguity in relation to preparing to enter a non-kinship placement, she was retained as a participant in the study.

OBTAINING CONSENT

The research study was reviewed and approved by an institutional review board at a Canadian university. Ethical considerations included, yet were not limited to, a description of the risks and benefits of the study, assurance of confidentiality, acknowledgment of participants' rights, and provisions that would be appropriated to protect the vulnerability of the participants. Approval from the host agency was sought and approved through the submission and rigorous review of a research proposal by the agency and a formal meeting with the agency's executive committee. Consent to participate in the study was sought through the children's legal guardians (i.e., their case managers) and the children themselves. An information package outlining the study (e.g., purpose and details of the study, consent form, and study information form) was sent to both case managers and children. Each package was authored and customized for its intended audience. The information packages for children were self-addressed (to personalize the invitation) and were only provided to children if the case manager first provided consent. This approach was to avoid any disappointment that might occur for children who wanted to participate in the study but did not have approval of their legal guardian. Additionally, children were also given an opportunity to decline to participate in the study despite their legal guardian's consent for them to participate. Ultimately, both parties were required to provide consent in order for a child to participate in the study. The care providers of the children who chose to participate in the study also received an information package outlining the details of the study.

DATA ANALYSIS

Children participated in a group workshop (phase one) and an individual semi-structured interview (phase two): data was collected during the latter phase of the study. (For more information on the research method, collected during the second phase of the research study, please refer to "The Voices" in the Preface). Consistent with the hermeneutic phenomenological analytic approach presented by Leonard (1994), data was analyzed through thematic analysis, identification of exemplars, and a search for paradigm cases. To assist with the first step of data analysis (i.e., thematic analysis), interviews were transcribed verbatim and checked for accuracy. The interviews were read multiple times to attain an overall understanding of the data collected. The data was entered into MAXQDA, a qualitative software, to assist with organizing the data for analysis. Interviews were microanalyzed (i.e., analysis of line-by-line coding) in a successive manner using open coding (i.e., assigning names to phenomena using a line-by-line coding system). Similar codes were grouped together in order to reflect categories that emerged from the data. These categories were held loosely and were considered flexible to change. As additional lines of inquiry related to the experience of transitioning into foster care arose, new categories were formed and were included in the interpretive plan. The categories were then further scrutinized to identify the various categorical dimensions that had emerged (i.e., distinguishing categories that are main categories from those that are subcategories). As analysis progressed, themes that emerged from the data were documented. The themes reflected the appraisals, values, and experiences that had been reported during the interviews. Memos were taken throughout analysis to reflect on the data and the categories and themes that were emerging. Exemplars arose from the analysis of participants' concerns, actions, and practices of specific events related to the research phenomena. These exemplars provided a rich description of children's lived experiences of the transition into foster care and were used to highlight key elements within themes. Common experiences were woven together to create paradigm cases (i.e., repetitive instances of specific patterns of meaning and an amalgamation of elements from various stories) that represented the participants' lived experience of the transition into foster care. Please see *Abigail's Story* in the Introduction for an example of a paradigm case that emerged from the research.

REDUCING BIAS

Reducing bias is a key criterion of hermeneutic phenomenological research (Khan, 2000). The steps that were taken to assist with bias reduction were an audit trail, critical reflection, advisory consultation, lived experience confirmation, and immersion in the hermeneutic circle. An audit trail, which included documentation on general reflections, methodological reflections, analytic reflections, and consultation reflections, was developed to reflect on daily events and decisions related to the research process.

Critical reflection, which involved reflections on the study design, concepts and categories emerging from the data, relevant background literature, and/or presuppositions, was reported exhaustively in the MAXQDA logbook. Any decisions related to the research process were documented in the logbook as well as in the respective section in the audit trail (i.e., methodological or analytic reflections). Consultations on the research questions, procedure, emerging codes and categories, axial coding, and interpretation occurred weekly with committee members. These meetings were particularly helpful to reflecting on the data and findings. Another approach to reduce bias involved providing participants with a summary of their interview and an opportunity to confirm the information that had been captured. In addition, the committee advisor reviewed the lived experiences and cross-referenced them with the transcriptions to verify that the summaries adequately and appropriately captured the information reported by the participants. Finally, constant engagement with the data in a dialectic process (i.e., recursively reflecting on the parts and whole of the lived experience text) was performed to immerse myself in a hermeneutic circle.

Appendix C

THE NEGLECTED TRANSITION: C.A.R.E. CHECKLIST

C.A.R.E. Checklist	Y/N
1.1 C.A.R.E. for Children's Foster Care Notification	
Is someone with whom the child is familiar present when the child is being notified that he or she is being placed into foster care?	
Have you introduced yourself to the child and explained who you are?	
Have you been sensitive to the child's feelings and provided an opportunity for the child to ask questions?	
1.2 C.A.R.E. for Children's Belongings	
Have you asked the child if there is anything that is important to him or her in the home that he or she would like to bring with him or her?	
(If applicable) Have you explained to the child why certain belongings of importance are not able to be transferred with him or her to his or her foster care placement?	
1.3 C.A.R.E. for Children's Experiences of Placement Reason Ambiguity	
Have you told the child why he or she has been placed into foster care, in an age-appropriate manner?	
Have you provided the child with an opportunity to ask any clarifying questions about why he or she has been placed into foster care?	
Have you told the child that he or she is not to blame for being placed into foster care?	
1.4 C.A.R.E. for Children's Preference for Parental Accompaniment	
Have you taken into consideration the child's feelings about the presence/absence of their family members during his or her placement into foster care?	
(If applicable) Have you told the child why his or her parents cannot accompany him or her to the foster care placement?	
(If applicable) Have you offered the child an opportunity to bring a personal belonging that reminds him or her of his or her loved ones?	
1.5 C.A.R.E. for Family Processing Time	
(If safe to do so) Have you provided the child with an opportunity to spend time with his or her family after receiving the notice that he or she is being removed from the home and before he or she is actually removed from the home?	
Have you given the child and family guidance regarding how to process the child's need to be removed from the home and efforts that will be made to keep the family relationships intact?	
1.6 C.A.R.E. for Children's Experiences of the Home Transfer	
Have you provided the child with sensitivity, compassion, and support while being transferred from the original home to the foster care placement?	

C.A.R.E. Checklist	Y/N
(If applicable and when possible) Have you asked the police officer, if at all possible, to arrive in citizen's attire?	
(If applicable) Have you inquired if a youth advocate has been assigned to the child during his or her transfer to their foster care placement?	
2.1 C.A.R.E. for Children's Experiences of Structural Ambiguity	
Have you provided the child with information about the foster care system and its purpose?	
Have you advised the child that efforts will be made for him or her to see his or her family again?	
2.2 C.A.R.E. for Children's Experiences of the Placement Route and Process	
Have you told the child where he or she is going and if there will be any location stops prior to his or her arrival to the foster care placement?	
If the child is being brought to a child welfare agency or other non-residential institution, have you notified the child that this is not where he or she will be residing?	
2.3 C.A.R.E. for Children's Experiences of Family Threat	
Have you advised the child about how his or her relationships with loved ones will be maintained?	
2.4 C.A.R.E. for Children's Basic Needs	
Have you advised the child that his or her basic needs will be met and how these needs will be met?	
Have you advised the child about which adults are responsible for meeting his or her needs and whom to ask questions about his or her needs being met?	
Have you provided the child with the opportunity to speak with a counselor or therapist about any concerns, fears, or emotions he or she may be experiencing?	
2.5 C.A.R.E. for Children's Experiences of School Threat	
Have all efforts been made to refrain from removing the child from his or her school?	
(If applicable) Have you notified the child that he or she has to attend a new school? Have efforts been made to maintain the child's relationships with peers and other individuals of importance at his or her former school?	
2.6 C.A.R.E. for Children's Experiences of Foster Care Benefits	
Have you informed the child of the benefits of foster care?	

C.A.R.E. Checklist	Y/N
3.1 C.A.R.E. for Children's Experiences of Placement Context Ambiguity	
Have you provided the child with a Care Entry package?	
Have you provided the child with information about his or her foster care residence and the people residing in the home?	
3.2 C.A.R.E. for Children's Preferences for Pets	
Have you advised the child if there are pets at the home where he or she will be living?	
Have you taken into consideration the child's feelings about pets when preparing him or her for his or her foster care placement?	
(If applicable) Have you addressed and attended to the child's potential fears about the home, people, or pets with whom he or she will be residing?	
3.3 C.A.R.E for Children's Experiences of Their Home Environment	
Have you introduced yourself to the child and welcomed him or her to the home?	
Have you provided the child with a tour of the foster care placement?	
Have you provided the child with an opportunity to ask questions about the home?	
Have you invited the child to "personalize" his or her room in some manner?	
3.4 C.A.R.E. for Children's Experiences of Household Rules	
Have you advised the child about the household rules and the purpose of each rule?	
Have you invited the child to co-create some of the household rules?	
Have you invited the child to ask questions about the rules and household expectations?	
3.5 C.A.R.E. for Children's Experiences of Foster Placement Adjustment	
Have you offered the child support in adjusting to his or her new environment?	
Have you provided the child with some time to adjust to his or her new environment before tasks and/or chores have been assigned to him or her?	
Have you invited the child to express what might assist him or her with adjusting to the home?	
3.6 C.A.R.E. for Sibling Connections in the Home	
(If applicable) Have you asked the child about his or her preferences about sharing a room with his or her sibling?	
(If applicable) Have you advised the child why he or she cannot share a room with his or her sibling?	

C.A.R.E. Checklist	Y/N
4.1 C.A.R.E. for a Relational Foundation of Security, Safety, and Trust	
Have you provided a safe and secure physical environment?	
Have you invited the child to share feedback about what changes could be made in the home environment to assist him or her with feeling more secure and safe?	
4.2 C.A.R.E. for a Welcoming Home Atmosphere	
Have you provided a warm welcome to the child?	
Have you advised the child that you are available to him or her at any time and are open to receiving questions and feedback from the child?	
4.3 C.A.R.E. for Equal Treatment of Children in the Home	
(If applicable) Do you treat the child equally to other children who are residing in the home?	
(If applicable) Have you provided the child with opportunities to express if he or she believes that there is unfair treatment between children in the home?	
(If applicable) Have you acknowledged and attended to the child's concerns about parental favoritism in a considerate, compassionate, and non-defensive manner?	
4.4 C.A.R.E. for Respectful Communication	
Do you communicate with the child in a respectful and non-condescending manner?	
4.5 C.A.R.E. for Constant Love and Support	
Do you frequently invite the child to speak about his or her needs, concerns, interests, and feelings?	
5.1 C.A.R.E. for Children's Experiences of Role Ambiguity	
Have you asked the child about his/her perceptions of family roles prior to and after entering foster care?	
Have you invited the child to discuss his or her feelings about any roles that he/she no longer performs/is unable to perform?	
Have you provided the child with opportunities to preserve healthy roles that are important to him or her?	
5.2 C.A.R.E. for Children's Interests and Commitments	
Have you asked the child about his or her interests?	
Have you made efforts to identify similar or shared interests with the child?	
Have you encouraged and supported the child in pursuing his or her interests?	
Have you actively invested in the child's interests?	

C.A.R.E. Checklist	Y/N
5.3 C.A.R.E. for Children's Friendships	
Have you provided the child with supports to assist him or her in maintaining previous friendships?	
Have you assisted the child in establishing new friendships?	
5.4 C.A.R.E. for Inviting, Involving, and Engaging Children in Decision-Making Opportunities	
Have you invited, involved, and engaged the child in decision-making that could affect him or her?	
5.5 C.A.R.E. for Children's Spiritual Beliefs	
Have you invited the child to openly discuss her or her spiritual beliefs?	
Have you made efforts to encourage and support the child in practicing and exploring his or her spiritual beliefs?	
5.6 C.A.R.E. for Children's Feelings	
Have you advised the child that his/her feelings are important and that you are available to listen to him or her when he/she would like to express these feelings?	
Have you provided the child with opportunities to express his or her feelings?	
(If applicable) Does the child have a therapist with whom he/she can speak when he or she is emotionally distressed?	
Does the child have an adequate social support network that he or she can draw from when he or she needs someone to speak with?	
6.1 C.A.R.E. for Children's Experiences of Temporal Ambiguity	
Have you provided the child with open and honest communication regarding the length of time he or she will be placed in foster care?	
(If applicable) Have you given the child opportunities to explain and discuss his or her feelings about the uncertainty of the length of time he or she will be in foster care?	
6.2 C.A.R.E. for Children's Experiences of Ambiguous Loss	
Have you invited the child to identify and discuss the losses that he or she is experiencing?	
Have you provided the child with opportunities to explore how she or he makes meaning of his or her current situation and losses?	
Have you invited the child to discuss how he or she is feeling about the losses he or she is experiencing?	
Have your made efforts to understand and attend to the child's losses, grief, and the effects these losses are having on him or her?	

C.A.R.E. Checklist	Y/N
(If applicable) Have you advised/reminded the child that efforts are being made to reunify him or her with his or her family?	
Have you advised/reminded the child that he or she is valued, significant, and has purpose in this world?	
6.3 C.A.R.E. for Family Visitations	
(If applicable) Have you notified the child that he or she will have visitations with his or her family members, including who will be visited, how often the visits will occur, and when and where the visits will take place?	
If the child is not permitted to have visitations with people of importance to him or her, have you advised the child of the reason for this decision?	
(If applicable) Have you asked the child if he/she would like to have visitations with his or her parents alone as well as shared visits with siblings?	
6.4 C.A.R.E. for Children's Healing and Coping Processes	
Have you acknowledged and validated the child's experiences of loss and grief?	
Have you encouraged, supported, and nurtured the child's healthy coping responses?	
Have you provided the child with opportunities to engage in healthy activities that can maintain connections with loved ones who are physically absent yet psychologically present?	
6.5 C.A.R.E. for the Healing Properties of Time	
Have you encouraged and supported the child daily and reminded him/her to take each day one step at a time?	

Appendix D

HEALING AFFIRMATIONS FOR CHILDREN
AND YOUTH IN FOSTER CARE

- I have a unique purpose in this world.
- I am loved unconditionally.
- I deserve to be happy.
- I am bigger than anything that ever happens to me.
- I am important.
- I am a good person.
- In all situations, I can choose peace.
- I am deserving of love.
- People see the good in me. I see the good in me.
- I will make mistakes and that is OK. I can learn from my mistakes.
- I am not alone.
- I believe in my abilities and my strengths.
- I love myself.
- I will express my feelings in a way that is healthy and helps me.
- I know I am loved.
- I believe in opportunities.
- It is OK to have feelings.
- My experiences do not define me. I define me.
- My feelings, ideas, and interests are important.
- People love and accept me for who I am.
- I am open to change.
- I am unique and lovable.
- I believe in myself.
- Love is the answer.

REFERENCES

Auden, J. M. (1995). Lessons on living from dying adolescents. In J. D. Morgan (Series Ed.) & D. W. Adams & E. J. Deveau (Vol. Eds.), *Beyond the innocence of childhood*, Vol. 2, *Helping children and adolescents cope with life-threatening illness and dying.* Amityville, NY: Baywood Publishing.

Benner, P. (1994). Introduction. In P. Benner (Ed.), *Interpretive phenomenology: Embodiment, caring, and ethics in health and illness* (pp. xiii–xxvii). Thousand Oaks, CA: Sage.

Blome, W. (1997). What happens to foster kids: Educational experiences of a random sample of foster care youth and a matched group of non-foster care youth. *Child and Adolescent Social Work Journal, 14*(1), 41–53.

Boss, P. (1999). *Ambiguous loss: Learning to live with unresolved grief.* Cambridge, MA: Harvard University Press.

Boss, P. (2006). *Loss, trauma, and resilience: Therapeutic work with ambiguous loss.* New York: W. W. Norton.

Boyd Webb, N. (Ed.). (2006). *Working with traumatized youth in child welfare.* New York: Guilford Press.

Bruskas, D. (2008). Children in foster care: A vulnerable population at risk. *Journal of Child and Adolescent Psychiatric Nursing, 21*(2), 70–77.

Butler, S., & Charles, M. (1999). 'The past, the present, but never the future': Thematic representations of fostering disruption. *Child and Family Social Work, 4*(1), 9–19.

Casey Family Programs. (2007). *Educating children in foster care: The McKinney-Vento and No Child Left Behind Acts.* Seattle, WA: Casey Family Programs.

Chambers, C., & Palmer, E. (2011). Educational stability for children in foster care. *Touro Law Review, 26*(4), 1103–1130.

Chow, C., & Sarin, R. K. (2002). Known, unknown, and unknowable certainties. *Theory and Decision, 52*, 127–138.

Courtney, M. E., Piliavin, I., Grogan-Kaylor, A., & Nesmith, A. (2001). Foster youth transitions to adulthood: A longitudinal view of youth leaving care. *Child Welfare, 80*(6), 685–717.

Cowan, P. A. (1991). Individual and family life transitions: A proposal for a new definition. In P. A. Cowan & M. Hetherington, M. (Eds.), *Family transitions.* (pp. 3–30). Hillsdale, NJ: Lawrence Erlbaum Associates.

DeSpelder, L. A., & Strickland, A. L. (2010). *The last dance: Encountering death and dying* (8th ed.). Boston, MA: McGraw Hill.

DiLorenzo, P., & Nix-Early, V. (2004). *Untapped anchor: A monograph exploring the role of spirituality in the lives of foster youth.* Retrieved April 29, 2011 from http://pccyfs.org/practice_resources/Final%20Monograph.pdf

Doka, K. J. (Ed.). (1989). *Disenfranchised grief: Recognizing hidden sorrow.* Lexington, MA: Lexington.

Doka, K. J. (2002). Introduction. In *Disenfranchised grief: New directions, challenges, and strategies* (pp. 5–22). Champaign, IL: Research Press.

Eagle, R. S. (1994). The separation experience of children in long-term care: Theory, research, and implications for practice. *American Journal of Orthopsychiatry, 64*, 421–434.

Edelstein, S., Burge, D., & Waterman, J. (2001). Helping foster parents cope with separation, loss, and grief. *Child Welfare, 80*(1), 5–25.

Fahlberg, V. (1991). *A child's journey through placement.* Indianapolis, IN: Perspectives Press.

Gilligan, R. (2001). *Promoting resilience: A resource guide on working with children in the care system.* London: British Agencies for Adoption and Fostering.

Herrick, M., & Piccus, W. (2005). Sibling connections: The importance of nurturing sibling bonds in the foster care system. *Children and Youth Services Review, 27*, 845–861.

Jackson, L., Roller White, C., O'Brien, K., DiLorenzo, P., Cathcart, E., Wolf, M., Bruskas, D., Pecora, P., Nix-Early, V., & Cabrera, J. (2010). Exploring spirituality among youth in foster care: Findings from the Casey Field Office Mental Health Study. *Child and Family Social Work, 15*, 107–117.

Janoff-Bulman, R. (1989). Assumptive worlds and the stress of traumatic events: Applications of the schema construct. *Social Cognition, 7*, 113–136.

Kauffman, J. (Ed.). (2002). *Loss of the assumptive world: A theory of traumatic loss.* New York: Brunner-Routledge.

Khan, D. L. (2000). Reducing bias. In M. Z. Cohen, D. L. Khan, & R. H. Stevens (Eds.), *Hermeneutic phenomenological research: A practical guide for nurse researchers* (pp. 85–99). Thousand Oaks, CA: Sage.

Kools, S. (1997). Adolescent identity development in foster care. *Family Relations, 46*(3), 263–271.

Lazarus, R. S., & Folkman, S. (1984). *Stress, appraisal, and coping.* New York: Springer.

Leathers, S. J. (2003). Parental visiting, conflicting allegiances, emotional and behavioral problems among foster children. *Family Relations, 52*(1), 53–63.

Lee, R., & Whiting, J. (2007). Foster children's expressions of ambiguous loss. *The American Journal of Family Therapy, 35*(5), 417–428.

Leonard, V. W. (1994). A Heideggerian phenomenological perspective on the concept of person. In P. Benner (Ed.), *Interpretive phenomenology: Embodiment, caring, and ethics in health and illness* (pp. 43–63). Thousand Oaks, CA: Sage.

Levine, S. (2006). *Unattended sorrow: Recovering from loss and reviving the heart.* Emmaus, PA: Rodale.

Mitchell, M. B. (2008). The transitioning into care project: Honouring children's lived experience of the foster care transition. (Doctoral dissertation). *ProQuest Dissertations and Theses* database (UMI No. NR47610).

Mitchell, M. B. (2014). *Voices and visions of SC youth in transition: A report of the survey of 19-year-old youth in foster care* [Brochure]. Columbia: University of South Carolina.

Mitchell, M. B. (in press). The family dance: Ambiguous loss, meaning-making, and the psychological family in foster care. *Journal of Family Theory and Review.*

Mitchell, M. B., Jones, T., & Renema, S. (2015). Will I make it on my own? Voices and visions of 17-year-old youth in transition. *Child and Adolescent Social Work, 32,* 291–300.

Mitchell, M. B., & Kuczynski, L. (2010). Does anyone know what is going on? Examining children's lived experience of the transition into foster care. *Children and Youth Services Review, 32,* 437–444.

Mitchell, M. B., Kuczynski, L., Tubbs, C. Y., & Ross, C. (2010). We care about care: Advice by children in care for children in care, foster parents, and child welfare workers about the transition into foster care. *Child and Family Social Work, 15*(2), 176–185.

Mitchell, M. B., Silver, C. F., & Ross, C. F. J. (2012). My hero, my friend: Exploring Honduran youths' lived experience of the God-Individual relationship. *International Journal of Children's Spirituality, 17*(2), 137–151.

Mitchell, M. B., Vann, L. H., & Jones, T. (2014). *A youth evaluation of the Chafee Independent Living Program in South Carolina: An analysis of the National Youth in Transition Database and Voices and Visions of SC Youth in Transition survey data for South Carolina (FFY2013).* (White paper). University of South Carolina, Columbia, SC: The Center for Child and Family Studies.

Neimeyer, R. (Ed.). (2001). *Meaning reconstruction and the experience of loss.* Washington, DC: American Psychology Association.

Nolen-Hoeksema, S., Parker, L. E., & Larson, J. (1994). Ruminative coping with depressed mood following loss. *Journal of Personality and Social Psychology, 67*(1), 92–104.

Palmer, S. E. (1996). Placement stability and inclusive practice in foster care: An empirical study. *Children and Youth Services Review, 18*(7), 589–601.

Parker, J., Rubin, K., Erath, S., Wojslawowicz, J., & Buskirk, A. (2006). Peer relationships, child development, and adjustment: A developmental psychopathology perspective. In D. Cicchetti & D. J. Cohen (Eds.), *Developmental psychopathology,* Vol. 1, *Theory and method* (2nd ed.) (pp. 419–493). Hoboken, NJ: John Wiley & Sons.

Parkes, C. M. (1971). Psycho-social transition: A field of study. *Social Science and Medicine, 5,* 101–115.

Piaget, J. (1930). *The child's conception of physical causality.* London: Rutledge.

Patterson, M. E. & Williams, D. R. (2002). Collecting and analyzing qualitative data: Hermeneutic principles, methods, and case examples. In D. R. Fesenmaier, J. T. O'Leary, and M. S. Uysal (Eds.), Vol. 9. *Advances in Tourism Applications Series* (pp. i–127). Champaign, IL: Sagamore Publishing, Inc.

Riggs, D., & Willsmore, S. (2012). Experiences of disenfranchised grief arising from the unplanned termination of a foster placement: An exploratory South Australian study. *Adoption & Fostering, 93*(2), 57–66.

Silverman, P. (2004). *Widow to widow: How the bereaved help one another* (2nd ed.). New York: Brunner-Routledge.

Simpson, J. (2012). Grief and loss: A social work perspective. *Journal of Loss and Trauma, 18*(1), 81–90.

Sinclair, I., Wilson, K., & Gibbs, I. (2005) *Foster placements: Why they succeed and why they fail.* London: Jessica Kingsley Publishers.

Stolorow, R. D. (2007). *Trauma and human existence: Autobiographical, psychoanalytic, and philosophical reflections.* New York: The Analytic Press.

Unrau, Y. A., Seita, J. R., & Putney, K. S. (2008). Former foster youth remember multiple placement moves: A journey of loss and hope. *Children and Youth Services Review, 30*(11), 1256–1266.

Urry, H. L., & Poey, A. P. (2008). Positive youth development & spirituality: From theory to research. In R. M. Lerner, R. W. Roeser, & E. Phelps (Eds.), *How religious/spiritual practices contribute to well-being* (pp. 145–163). Pennsylvania: Templeton Foundation Press.

Van Bijleveld, G., Dedding, C., & Bunders-Aelen, J. (2015). Children's and young people's participation within child welfare and child protection services: A state-of-the-art review. *Child and Family Social Work, 20*, 129–138.

Vis, S. A., Strandbu, A., Holtan, A., & Thomas, N. (2011). Participation and health: A research review of child participation in planning and decision-making. *Child and Family Social Work, 16*, 325–335.

Walsh, K. (2012). *Grief and loss: Theories and skills for the helping professions* (rev. ed.). New York: Pearson.

Ward, M. (1984). Sibling ties in foster care and adoption planning. *Child Welfare, 63*(4), 321–332.

Whiting, J. B., & Lee, R. E. (2003). Voices from the system: A qualitative study of foster children's stories. *Family Relations, 52*, 288–295.

Worden, J. W. (2005, April). *Child bereavement study.* Paper presented at the annual conference of Bereaved Families of Ontario-Waterloo Region, Waterloo, ON.

Yule, W., & Williams, R. (1990). Post-traumatic stress reactions in children. *Journal of Traumatic Stress, 3*(2), 279–295.